Praying the Stations
of the Cross

PRAYING THE STATIONS OF THE CROSS

OF THE CROSS

Finding Hope in a Weary Land

Margaret Adams Parker
and Katherine Sonderegger

WILLIAM B. EERDMANS PUBLISHING COMPANY
GRAND RAPIDS, MICHIGAN

Wm. B. Eerdmans Publishing Co.
4035 Park East Court SE, Grand Rapids, Michigan 49546
www.eerdmans.com

25 24 23 22 21 20 19   1 2 3 4 5 6 7

ISBN 978-0-8028-7664-5

Library of Congress Cataloging-in-Publication Data

A catalog record for this book is available from the Library of Congress.

For Lynne and Sandy,
for Caroline and Rebecca,
and
for the parishioners, staff, and clergy of
St. Mary's Episcopal Church, Arlington, Virginia

How precious is your steadfast love, O God!
All people may take refuge in the shadow of your wings.
PSALM 36:7

Contents

Acknowledgments

As we note in the introduction, we have worked singly and collaboratively on this book. Our work on the individual pieces, and on the assembled whole, has been a labor of love over many years, and we are grateful to the many people who have offered support to us and to this project.

The artist: I am grateful to my husband, Bruce, who has lovingly encouraged my work and (for this project) provided the additional assistance of his woodworking skills, piecing the woodcut blocks together out of poplar planks; to our son, Ross, who was always available to critique with a discerning and honest eye; and to our daughter, Margaret, for her ready enthusiasm.

I have relied on dear theological colleagues for their unfailing appreciation of my own art and of the significance of the arts in the life of the church: Steve Cook, Ellen Davis (with whom I collaborated on an earlier volume of text and image, a happy model for the current book), Joyce and Ray Glover, Kathy Grieb, and Bill Stafford (whose hands served as the model for Christ's hands in the *Ecce Homo*.) And our VTS dean, Ian Markham, has likewise supported my work.

My community of artist friends, among them Carole Nelson, Ellen and Max-Karl Winkler, and Judith Winshel, have offered much-needed comradeship, with the pleasures of mutual critique and shop talk, along the way; and Heidi Christensen, Lee Newman, and Deborah Sokolove, who bridge the worlds of sanctuary and studio, have generously afforded me their help and insight. John Baker and Rosemari Sullivan provided me the invaluable experience of exhibiting and teaching about the Stations in their parishes. And Jude Harmon, Mary Norton, and Jill Williams continue to be helpful and perceptive readers of my work.

I owe special thanks to countless friends among the parishioners, staff, and clergy of St. Mary's Episcopal Church in Arlington, Virginia. I name with gratitude Jane Drown for her perceptive eye; Carol Kurz and the women's group for their eagerness to pray our Stations service; Angela Shafran for her gracious appreciation for these Stations images; and Barbara Stafford for her ready wit and enthusiasm. Jane Shafran has carefully and prayerfully hung the Stations every Lent, and Pam Frick has been a steady friend and companion through all seasons; these dear friends, like Anna, have served long and selflessly in the temple. And Andrew Merrow has provided the faithful witness, generosity of spirit, and steady leadership that have helped make St. Mary's parish a home that shelters our congregation and sends us out into the world in witness to the gospel.

Finally, I am grateful to my dear friend and collaborator, Kate Sonderegger, whose depth, creativity, and integrity as a scholar, clarity and kindness as a teacher, wisdom and faithfulness as a priest, and loving affirmation as a friend and companion are immeasurable gifts from which I learn every day.

The preacher: Preaching is a task and gift of the whole church; it is never done alone. I am keenly aware of the many teachers, voices, congregations, and readers who have strengthened me as a preacher, guided me when I strayed, and generously supported me as I undertook this wonderful and weighty office. I learned to recognize what a sermon is—this distinct genre of the church—and what the marks of strong biblical preaching are from the pastors and people of the First Presbyterian

Acknowledgments

Church in Marquette, Michigan, my hometown. I remember with special
gratitude the preaching of the Rev. Richard Unsworth, chaplain at Smith
College, who taught me the moral force and power of the pulpit. Yale
Divinity School was filled with strong and courageous preachers; they
stood under the Word of God in such a way that the troubled waters of
the 1970s were addressed, chastened, and illumined by holy Scripture.
Anyone who heard the Rev. William Sloane Coffin in those days knows
what biblical, prophetic preaching is all about. I am now surrounded
by faithful, thoughtful, and creative preachers—the rector, Fr. Andrew
Merrow (one of our church's finest preachers), and associate priests at St.
Mary's Church, Arlington, as well as the students and faculty at Virginia
Theological Seminary—and am privileged to sit under their pulpit, and
receive that word, in season and out. I am grateful to them for breaking
open the Word for me and for allowing me to preach in their midst. The
deans of our chapel—the Rev. Dr. Ian Markham and the Rev. Dr. Ruth-
anna Hooke—deserve my special thanks for organizing the complex life
that is daily seminary worship and for making preaching a central act of
every Holy Eucharist.

Of course, preaching is not all auditory! The works of theology in-
struct us about the preached word as little else can do. I want to pay
special tribute to the writing of Karl Barth. I have found over the years
that I cannot agree with him everywhere and always—he may not even
have desired this complete agreement, had he known of it. But far more
than that, I have found in his words, his theological passion and confidence, his matchless dynamism and radiant hope, a sermon, lavished
over four volumes and some 10,000 pages. Holy Scripture lives in these
pages. Should anyone want a brief introduction to Barth as theological
preacher, I would encourage him or her to turn to Barth's treatment of the
resurrection as a "coming from death." It's Barth at his most homiletic and
his most theological; his words breathe the glorious air of early Easter
morning. See *Church Dogmatics*, volume IV, part 2, paragraph 64.2, the
"Homecoming of the Son of Man," pp. 151–54.

And in the end, but not at all least, I would like to honor my coauthor Peggy Parker. She is the architect of the whole and has shown me how wood panel and carving tool can illumine holy Scripture and teach me more deeply the Mystery who is Christ. Peggy's work is consistently and richly biblical, passionate in joy and lament, remarkably fresh and timeless. I am honored to be counted among her friends.

Together we thank our editor at Eerdmans, Jenny Hoffman, for her responsiveness and gracious collegiality. And we convey our particular gratitude to Lil Copan, whose editorial suggestions strengthened this book immensely and whose advocacy made its publication possible.

We hope that our book will carry forward an ancient tradition, renewing it for future generations. With that link between past and future in mind, we dedicate our book to dear friends, Sandy and Lynne, now rejoicing on another shore and in a greater Light; to dear young ones, Caroline and Rebecca, growing up under the church's protecting wings; and to St. Mary's, the parish that sustains and strengthens us.

Introduction

As a deer longs for flowing streams,
*   so my soul longs for you, O God.*
My soul thirsts for God,
*   for the living God.*

PSALM 42:1–2

Praying the Stations of the Cross is among the most ancient of spiritual disciplines, a practice that stretches back to the early centuries of the church. We often consider the Stations a penitential practice, one most appropriate for Lent and—especially—Holy Week. Yet, truly, the Stations of the Cross have no season. Suffering, sorrow, injustice, confusion, and death can touch any of us, at any time; the shadow of the cross lies even across the infant in the stable. The Stations can offer consolation and comfort when we are grieving; healing and restoration when we are parched; inspiration and guidance when we are searching or lost or simply beset by the turmoil and temptation, isolation and insecurity that unsettle all our lives.

The Stations speak to us in the political, social, and economic conflicts and dilemmas that descend on us all. And to a culture, to individuals, and, sadly, even to a church that scrupulously turn away from the reality of death, the Stations speak an important word about that final frontier.

But even more, the Stations offer a spiritual practice that can refresh us at those times when our souls are parched for God's presence in our lives, when—like the deer—we long for flowing water. And in taking up this discipline we join all those on the pilgrim way—mystics, saints, martyrs, truth- and justice-seekers, and those in that great cloud of witnesses, unnamed and unnumbered—who have drawn comfort in their lives, in their work, and most especially in their suffering from entering into Christ's own Way of Sorrows.

This book invites us to join those witnesses, entering into the Stations through image, prayer, and reflection. It is written for anyone coming new to the Stations, as well as for those long familiar with the practice. It is for individuals, for small groups, for entire congregations. It can be taken up for a season, at a particular moment of need, or as a devotion of a lifetime. It aims to connect each of us, in a life-giving way, with the suffering that Christ took on for our sake; it is designed to slake our thirst.

The first two sections of our book offer opportunities for reflection and prayer; the final section offers material for further study.

Bearing Witness through the Stations of the Cross

The book opens with an overview of the Stations and their theological meaning, scriptural significance, and pastoral dimensions—exploring the ways in which the Stations have sustained fellow witnesses through the centuries and throughout the liturgical year. We continue with reflections on Christ's passion. The selection gathered here—from centuries of word, image, and song—draws us into the prayer of Christian witnesses ancient and modern: from the medieval mystic Julian of Norwich to the twentieth-century martyr Martin Luther King Jr.; from Geoffrey Studdert Kennedy, Anglican priest and World War I chaplain, to Sundar Singh, the wandering Punjabi Anglican evangelical; from a wrenching

2

Latin American depiction of the crucifixion to the plain wooden crosses carried in 1946 from across Europe into the ancient medieval cathedral at Vézaley, France; from the spirituals of enslaved Africans to the sturdy hymnody of Reformation congregations. This section concludes with a brief history of the Stations, followed by suggestions for incorporating the Stations into our lives by adapting the Stations to the needs of particular groups or individuals, occasions or aims.

Praying the Stations

For each Station, we provide a spare and simple liturgy of Scripture and prayer, chant and silence; a graphically powerful woodcut image; and a theologically significant reflection. Together these elements provide a vivid and sometimes stark encounter with the meaning of the crucifixion: they draw us into the biblical narrative to engage some of the great questions of our lives and of our faith—among them, suffering, doubt, and darkness—and remind us as well of our steadfast hope for redemption and resurrection. As we walk the Way of the Cross we recall *all* those for whom Jesus was slain, including every one of us, in our sin and brokenness. The Stations point to the great hope of sinners: redeemed and freed, we are strengthened to serve Christ in his work in the world.

Resources for Further Study

In our final section we explore the nature of our work—as artist and as preacher—anticipating the kinds of questions we are often asked: *How long did it take you to make this image? How did you prepare to write that sermon?* We also address the deeper query, *Why do you do this?* In our artist's afterword and preacher's afterword we write about the ways we have been called to our vocations; we offer details about our training;

and we speak as well about the ongoing task (more correctly, the ongoing pleasure) of learning and preparation. We hope that these essays may encourage those who would take up similar work. We conclude with an annotated list of books that we have found particularly helpful.

One final note: we have worked on aspects of this book both singly and collaboratively. Margaret Adams Parker created the woodcut images. The theological reflections are drawn from Katherine Sonderegger's sermons and papers, which Parker edited and shaped to respond to the Stations. Parker wrote the introductory sections and the artist's afterword; Sonderegger wrote the preacher's afterword as well as the opening and closing prayers for our Stations service. Each of us contributed to the resources for further study, and we worked together on the texts and prayers for the Stations service.

Our hope and prayer is that these reflections, images, prayers, and passages from Scripture will bear fruit in all our hearts and minds, as well as in our actions, as we live more fully into our call to bear witness. May Christ meet you here, on the great pilgrim road of humankind.

In the name of our incarnate, crucified, and risen Lord,

MARGARET ADAMS PARKER
KATHERINE SONDEREGGER

¦ ¦ ¦ ¦ ¦ ¦ ¦ ¦ ¦ ¦ ¦ ¦ ¦ ¦

Bearing Witness through the Stations of the Cross

You are witnesses of these things.

LUKE 24:48

I want to know Christ and the power of his resurrection and the sharing of his sufferings by becoming like him in his death, if somehow I may attain the resurrection from the dead.

PHILIPPIANS 3:10–11

[We always carry] in the body the death of Jesus, so that the life of Jesus may also be made visible in our bodies. For while we live, we are always being given up to death for Jesus' sake, so that the life of Jesus may be made visible in our mortal flesh.

2 CORINTHIANS 4:10–11

Why the Stations

Countless pilgrims have walked and prayed the Stations of the Cross. We imagine that great cloud of witnesses, moving across centuries and cultures. We glimpse them in the winding streets of Jerusalem, in magnificent cathedrals of Europe, in dusty villages in South America. They are rich and poor, young and elderly, vigorous and dying, joyous and heartsick. They pray beside images resplendent in gold and rich color, in front of stark depictions in wood and unbaked clay, with Stations marked by numbers only. They speak and chant and pray in a myriad of languages. They weep. They stand silent. It is remarkable and moving to think of all of these worshipers—in ways so many and so varied—bearing witness to Jesus's atoning work.

Today the practice of the Stations, for centuries primarily a devotion for Roman Catholics, has spread into the other liturgical denominations and even beyond. It takes many forms, visually and liturgically, from the sparest set of recitations to the most ornate combination of images, texts, and hymns. But to some Christians the practice can seem strange, bizarre, or even offensive, a kind of lugubrious piety with the puzzling addition of nonbiblical scenes. Why would the Stations dwell on this suffering, offering prayers that often seem to focus on Christ's wounds? What is the spiritual and theological merit of the Stations? And how can a valid spiritual discipline include six (out of fourteen) scenes that are absent from the New Testament accounts of Christ's passion?

What might help us understand, and enter into, the practice of the Stations? We might imagine someone we love walking to his execution, or living through her final days with cancer. How dreadful is the death that takes place alone, unwatched, unwept! Knowing this, we might want to be with that friend, no matter how difficult the experience; we might want to remain to the very end, as witness, as loving support. Or we might wish to stay away, frightened, or repelled, or simply immobilized. For whether or not we have witnessed death, we understand its urgency; death cannot leave us indifferent.

In walking the Stations of the Cross, we accompany Jesus on his journey to death, his Via Dolorosa. This devotion allows us—whether or not we have attended another death, whether we were reluctant or willing—to stand as witness to this *one* death: we watch as Christ lifts the cross, wince as his hands are pierced, reach out to touch his body as it comes down from the cross.

And we may receive this gracious spiritual exchange as well: entering into Christ's sorrows may open our minds and hearts to the suffering of those around us. We remember Christ's identification with the sick and the lost: *Just as you did it to one of the least of these who are members of my family, you did it to me* (Matthew 25:40). These are the words Mother Teresa of Calcutta cited as a beacon in her ministry: "I see Jesus in every human being. I say to myself, this is hungry Jesus, I must feed him. This is sick Jesus. This one has leprosy or gangrene; I must wash him and tend to him. I serve because I love Jesus." And in much the same way praying the Stations can enlarge our sympathy for those who suffer, strengthening our spirits to serve among them.

Even more, the Stations of the Cross place all of us in the position of the original disciples and crowds and leaders who saw with their own eyes the earthly Jesus. In these images Christ's divinity is hidden under the veil of his flesh while his humanity is set before us, directly: we see with our own eyes the man Jesus, who stands before us, even as he did before those Galileans and Judeans of long ago. We see Christ as his contemporaries saw him: a Son of Man, a teacher and healer and miracle worker set on a course to Jerusalem, a course of suffering and death.

When we stand before these images of Christ in Jerusalem—his trial, his torment and betrayal, his bearing of the cross and falling under its weight, his suffering and death—we might find welling up in ourselves the responses of disciples and soldiers and passersby gathered for the Passover feast, so many centuries ago. Perhaps we are scandalized that this suffering man claimed to be God. Perhaps we find ourselves calling for him to come down from his cross and save himself. Perhaps we take our place under his cross, or among those who desert and flee. Perhaps the suffering does not touch us at all this day: we are passing by and we have seen all this many times before. Or perhaps this time the confession of the Roman soldier springs to our lips: *Truly this man was God's Son!* (Matthew 27:54). And only by seeing with our own eyes the broken humanity of Jesus can we articulate the astonishing claim of the Christian faith: in this obedient and dying son of Israel we see, by grace, the incarnate Son of God. The artist teaches us this gospel as no other theologian can.

Finally, Scripture and tradition meet in these Stations. True, only eight of the fourteen Stations depict scenes explicitly depicted in the Gospels' passion narrative. But we might consider these "nonbiblical" scenes as analogous to the kind of lovely expansion and elaboration (what the rabbinic tradition terms "midrash") that we find in our Christmas hymns. The cattle who wake the infant with their lowing are nowhere mentioned in the infancy narratives. Nor do we find in Scripture any description of the "cold of winter," a phrase from that most beautiful medieval text "Lo, How a Rose E'er Blooming." And Jesse Edgar Middleton's hymn text sets the story among Native American peoples, envisioning the Christ child wrapped in a "ragged robe of rabbit skin" and attended by "chiefs" who bring him gifts of "fox and beaver pelt." In these, as in many other beloved hymns, the texts express a tradition of devotion; around the edges of the biblical narrative they stitch tales that may picture a familiar setting, in this way helping to draw us into the narrative to stand before the holy child.

But even more significantly, the texts that accompany these six Stations follow a centuries-old tradition of drawing from the Old Testament to comment on or prefigure events in the New Testament. We see this first within Scripture itself. Jesus, worshiping in the synagogue in his hometown of Nazareth, reads from the prophet Isaiah to speak of his own ministry:

> The Spirit of the Lord is upon me,
>   because he has anointed me to bring good news to the poor.
> He has sent me to proclaim release to the captives
>   and recovery of sight to the blind,
>   to let the oppressed go free,
> to proclaim the year of the Lord's favor.
>
> (Luke 4:18–19, paraphrase of Isaiah 61:1–2)

He concludes with these words: *Today this scripture has been fulfilled in your hearing* (Luke 4:21). In the same way, in John's Gospel, Jesus cites Numbers 21:9 as the sign of the crucified Savior: *And just as Moses lifted up the serpent in the wilderness, so must the Son of Man be lifted up, that whoever believes in him may have eternal life* (John 3:14–15).

And early biblical commentators expanded on this tradition, citing Old Testament scenes to prefigure the New Testament narrative. Our Sunday lectionaries draw upon many of these pairings of Old and New Testament, especially in the season of Lent. The Suffering Servant song in Isaiah 53:1–12 is the most familiar of these: *He was despised and rejected by others* . . . (Isaiah 53:3). This tradition of typology occurs in visual form as well. On each page of the medieval *Biblia Pauperum* (*The Bible of the Poor*), images from the Old Testament bracket a central image from the New Testament: the manna in the wilderness is juxtaposed with the Last

Supper, the near-sacrifice of Isaac with Christ's crucifixion. And cycles of stained-glass windows, such as those in Chartres and Canterbury, depict the unity of the two Testaments through the pattern of typology, figure, and fulfillment.

Stations of the Cross liturgies often call upon this same kind of pairing. Jeremiah 31:15 most often accompanies Station XIII, the Pietà (Mary's lament over the body of her son):

> A voice is heard in Ramah,
> lamentation and bitter weeping.
> Rachel is weeping for her children . . .

And the verses that typically comment on Stations III, VII, and IX (where Christ falls under the weight of the cross) are drawn from the Suffering Servant songs mentioned above:

> By a perversion of justice he was taken away.
> Who could have imagined his future?
> For he was cut off from the land of the living,
> stricken for the transgression of my people.
>
> (Isaiah 53:8)

Or from Psalm 22:

> I am poured out like water,
> and all my bones are out of joint;
> my heart is like wax;
> it is melted within my breast;
> my mouth is dried up like a potsherd,
> and my tongue sticks to my jaws;
> you lay me in the dust of death.
>
> (Psalm 22:14–15)

When we pray the Stations we stand in a long tradition of imagining and entering into Christ's sufferings; of joining prophetic texts with Gospel narrative, Israel's deliverance with the world's redemption; of linking the passion with the pain and sorrow, darkness and injustice of our own day.

Passion Meditations in Word, Image, and Song

We wrote this book out of a conviction that contemplating Christ's passion can be a life-affirming practice. For those coming new to the Stations it might be helpful to look back over the many ways other Christians over the centuries have reflected on our Lord's Via Dolorosa. These meditations have taken many forms—word, image, and song—and offer different ways of understanding the passion. Some reflections speak of the ways in which Christ stands beside all those who suffer; others remind us that we are to see him in every sorrowing face that we encounter; still others offer Christ's suffering as an example to us to take up our own cross; others recall that our own sins have crucified the Lord, even while his very suffering atones for our sins; some find that all of Christ's life is embodied in the cross; others that the cross is the gateway to resurrection life. But woven through all these ways of considering the passion is the basic theological understanding that incarnation, passion, and resurrection are not to be separated from one other. It is simply not true that the Stations' only message for us is that of suffering.

Grünewald's giant triptych, the *Isenheim Altarpiece* (1511), is a powerful instance of passion images offering consolation to the sick and dying, the promise of life renewed after death. This stark and compelling work, a complex series of overlapping panels that includes sculpture as well as paintings, was commissioned for a hospice ministering to victims of the disfiguring and invariably fatal lesions of ergotism ("St. Anthony's fire," a disease of the poor who subsisted on bread infected with the ergot mold). Patients viewing the altarpiece would have been comforted by the image of the crucified Christ: with his hands and feet knotted in pain, his body a gangrenous green, his flesh scored with the lesions of thorn and cudgel and lash, he shared these sufferers' festering wounds. And the image of the resurrected Christ—flesh cleansed and healed—reassured the dying that they, too, would be whole in the resurrection.

The identification of Christ's suffering with our own pain is marked in the images of oppressed or enslaved peoples. Edilberto Merida's *Peruvian Crucifix* (1970s) depicts the crucified Lord as a tortured peasant. Tellingly, the wrenching clay sculpture is the cover image of Gustavo Gutiérrez's groundbreaking work, *A Theology of Liberation*. Fritz Eichenberg, in his *Crucifixion* from *Dance of Death* (1980), represents the crucified Christ as a Holocaust victim: a ragged figure, head encircled with a crown of barbed wire, hangs from a cross while Death, clothed in a Nazi uniform, stands guard on the other side of a barbed-wire barricade. A plaque records the sites of Nazi death camps, among them Auschwitz, Treblinka, Buchenwald, Bergen-Belsen. And at the end of the list is Golgotha. William Johnson, an African American artist working in the early twentieth century, paints the *Three Marys* (c. 1939–40) as dark-skinned women lifting their hands in lamentation for a black Christ hanging on the cross above them. A more recent piece by Hilary Garang Deng, an Anglican bishop in the stark land that is now South Sudan, a land riven for decades by conflict and massacre, is a woodcut print of a Christ (2000) from his own Dinka tribe: a dark face, beautiful and sorrowful, head crowned with thorns.

Images do not need to depict Christ's crucifixion to help us understand the passion. Rembrandt, in the works of his maturity, is one of the greatest visual interpreters of Scripture. But as a young man he was brash and ambitious, impressing us with his virtuosity rather than his depth. He was transformed, at least in part, by bearing witness to the suffering and death of his wife, Saskia, which he records in a heartbreaking series of images. We see her first as a winsome girl, newly betrothed at twenty-one (1633). Married the next year, she bore four children, only one of whom lived past infancy. Rembrandt's drawings often show Saskia in bed, sick, weary, and frightened. In a final image, an etching scarcely three inches square, the artist depicts his wife with the features of an old woman. She would die the next year, at the age of thirty (1642). Rembrandt brings this awareness of the fragility and holiness of life to his depictions of those he sees on the streets around him and infuses his biblical scenes with this same compassion and understanding.

Writers also, in this same way, enjoin us to see Christ in the faces of those who suffer. Geoffrey Studdert Kennedy, an Anglican priest and a chaplain in World War I, recalls an incident that changed his life. Under fire and running toward the front lines, he stumbled over an "undersized, underfed German boy," sprawled on the ground, fatally wounded:

> It seemed to me that the boy disappeared and in his place there lay the Christ upon His Cross, and cried, "Inasmuch as ye have done it unto the least of these my little ones you have done it unto me." From that moment on I never saw a battlefield as anything but a Crucifix. From that moment on I never saw the world as anything but a Crucifix. I see the Cross set up in every slum, in every filthy overcrowded quarter, in every vulgar flaring street that speaks of luxury and waste of life. I see Him staring up at me from the pages of the newspaper that tells of a tortured, lost, bewildered world.

Studdert Kennedy concludes his poem "High and Lifted Up" with a powerful affirmation of the link between that vision and our salvation:

> High and lifted up, I see Him on the eternal Calvary,
> And two piercèd hands are stretching east and west o'er land and
> sea.

On my knees I fall and worship that great Cross that shines above,
For the very God of Heaven is not Power, but Power of Love.

Sundar Singh, the Punjabi Anglican whose ministry in the early
twentieth century called him to wander, evangelizing, through North
India, also connected visions of the cross with God's love. Driven by
a storm into a cave in Nepal, suffering from fatigue as well as "extreme
hunger and thirst," Singh experienced the cave as "the lap of God." He
saw all the stages of the passion in a vision, understanding then that "the
Cross lifts those who lift it. It carries them to the streams of peace in this
world (which is full of pain) and it takes to heaven those who follow
Christ by lifting the Cross."

Could Singh have known the *Showings* of the medieval mystic Julian of Norwich? Unlikely. Yet Singh's words resonate with Dame Julian's
meditations. Julian dwells at length on Christ's suffering, revealed to her
at a moment of great sickness. She sees the blood flowing copiously from
his wounds. She enters Christ's body through those wounds. And she understands herself as clothed in Christ's body and his love. For both Singh
and Julian, a mystical experience of Christ's suffering is transfigured into
an awareness of God's abundant and overflowing love.

Tellingly, Martin Luther King Jr. gave the title *Strength to Love* to
his volume of collected sermons. King fulfilled in his ministry his com-
mitment to nonviolence and love as a means of reconciliation and social
justice; throughout his life—and with his death—he counted the cost.
King was keenly aware of the risks of his kind of discipleship. In his 1954
sermon "Transformed Non-Conformity," King took as his text Paul's ad-
monition in Romans 12:2 (in the King James Version), *Be not conformed
to this world*:

Honesty impels me to admit that transformed nonconformity,
which is always costly and never altogether comfortable, may
mean walking through the valley of the shadow of suffering, losing

a job, or having a six-year-old daughter ask, "Daddy, why do you have to go to jail so much?" But we are gravely mistaken to think that Christianity protects us from the pain and agony of mortal existence. Christianity has always insisted that the cross we bear precedes the crown we wear. To be a Christian, one must take up his cross, with all of its difficulties and agonizing and tragedy-packed content, and carry it until that very cross leaves its marks upon us and redeems us to that more excellent way which comes only through suffering.

Hymns, with their fusion of rhythm, melody, and text, offer a particularly powerful means of meditation on the passion. The great spiritual "Were You There When They Crucified My Lord?" sets us at the foot of the cross. Hymns such as this one, rooted in the mourning songs chanted in the "hush harbors" where slaves worshiped in secret, are a communal lament rising out of the suffering of enslaved peoples. As with those who viewed Grünewald's *Crucifixion*, these worshipers found in the figure of the crucified Lord consolation in their sorrow, strength for resistance, and hope in the world to come.

In his great *St. Matthew Passion*, J. S. Bach uses Hans Leo Hassler's *Passion Chorale* as a repeated theme, setting the melody to five different hymn texts. The most familiar of these texts is Paul Gerhardt's *O Sacred Head, Sore Wounded*, which has become a beloved Passiontide hymn. Singing the words, we mourn the dead Christ and thank him for our salvation, pleading in passionate language:

Ah, me, for whom thou diest, hide not so far thy grace:
Show me, O Love most highest, the brightness of thy face.

In a similar vein, Fred Pratt Green's hymn text "To Mock Your Reign, O Dearest Lord" describes the "grim charade" of the passion. Trusting that Christ's sorrows will "heal our own," he addresses Christ directly, expressing confidence that, "though we merit blame, you will your robe of mercy throw around our naked shame."

These meditations, in word, song, and image, invoke Christ's suffering but also his great love and forgiveness, extending a message of hope. The Community of the Cross of Nails, founded at England's Coventry Cathedral, focuses on just this kind of Christ-like reconciliation. The society was founded directly after the destruction of Coventry's great medieval cathedral by German bombers on November 14, 1940. The provost, Dick Howard, standing the next day in the rubble of the burned cathedral, picked up three of the long medieval roofing nails and tied them together into a cross. And on the broken sanctuary wall he wrote: "Father forgive." Christ's words from the cross anchor the Coventry Litany of Reconciliation and inspired the formation of the Community of the Cross of Nails. Originally focused on reconciliation between England and Germany, the community now includes 170 partners in such regions as Iraq, Ukraine, Israel/Palestine, and Sudan.

There is no way to cite more than a small fraction of the ways in which Christians through the centuries have meditated on Christ's suffering and death. The cross of Christ is both balm and direction, for Christ is both the Truth and the Way. Those touched by this crucified One follow that way, walking in his steps, seeing the world through his eyes. When we join his company, not one stone remains on another; everything is made new. We are sent, even as he is sent, into a suffering and unjust world, and we fight under his banner. In the way of the cross, his sorrow becomes ours, but even more, his victory becomes ours as well. We might end simply with our Lord's own words, summing up his passion and our own forgiveness: *Father, forgive them; for they do not know what they are doing* (Luke 23:34).

A History of the Stations

It is important to understand the origins of the Stations, for this great spiritual practice has sustained Christians since the early days of the church. Rooted in Christ's own journey to the cross, the Stations gained prominence as a result of Jerusalem's centrality for Christianity from the fourth century through the Middle Ages. While the political and ecclesial power of the Christian church had moved to Rome and Constantinople, Jerusalem remained its spiritual center.

It was Constantine, the first emperor of the Christian era, who reaffirmed Jerusalem's preeminence, transforming a Roman city into a center of Christian worship and establishing it as a major pilgrimage site. In 325 the emperor built the Church of the Holy Sepulchre to stand over the very places where, by tradition, Jesus was crucified and buried. At that same time the empress Helena, Constantine's mother, traveled to Jerusalem, establishing other churches and charitable foundations, and, according to tradition, discovered the remains of the true cross. She was one among many who traveled to Jerusalem to view the places of Christ's passion. St. Jerome (342–420), who lived in the Holy Land during the later years of his life, noted that pilgrims to Jerusalem would customarily retrace Jesus's journey to the cross. At each site they would stop (*station* is derived from the Latin *statum* for standing still) and meditate on the events of the passion. Egeria, a Galician woman who visited the holy sites between 381 and 384, recorded a Holy Week procession that began at the Garden of Gethsemane and wound its way into the city, with the pilgrims stopping to hear passages from Scripture, sing, and pray. Travelers took these practices home, and as early as the fifth century the Church of San Stefano in Bologna, Italy, boasted a set of Stations.

By the Middle Ages, European pilgrimage to the Holy Land had become common, although astonishingly rigorous. Pilgrims traveled on foot, by mule, or on horseback, with part of the trip often taken in chancy voyages over the Mediterranean in even more chancy small vessels. Many pilgrims never reached the Holy Land; others died on the return journey. And once in Jerusalem, they might encounter a troubled landscape. During many of the centuries from Constantine's reign through the late Middle Ages, Jerusalem was under Muslim rule. There were long periods when Christian pilgrims were welcomed (most notably under Saladin in the late twelfth century and Suleiman the Magnificent in the early sixteenth century). But other rulers merely tolerated Christians, while under others pilgrims were forbidden outright.

Franciscan friars, who were appointed "Guardians of the Holy Land" in 1342 by Pope Clement VI, shepherded medieval Christians through the streets of Jerusalem. Like all good tour guides, the Franciscans developed an itinerary so that visitors might tour the holy sites systematically. From surviving medieval journals we know that most pilgrims spent ten to fourteen days in Jerusalem. They visited sites such as the house of Dives, the house of Caiaphas, the palace of Annas, Herod's mansion, and the Mount of Olives. As the culmination of their visit, they would walk the Via Dolorosa, the Way of Sorrows, stopping to pray at Stations along the way.

Modern-day Franciscans (designated to this day as Guardians of the Holy Land) still lead pilgrims along that same medieval way, stopping at each Station to chant and pray. The way through these narrow streets is most likely not the historical Via Dolorosa. But in the wise words of one of the Sisters of Zion (whose convent and pilgrim's hostel is located at the

Ecce Homo arch, along the Via Dolorosa), centuries of prayers and tears have sanctified these places; Christ is here, whether or not the earthly Jesus walked on just these stones, standing before Pilate and lamenting over the women of Jerusalem.

What mattered for pilgrims—from the earliest centuries through today—was the act of standing witness to the suffering Christ endured. This also inspired them to replicate the sites at home. Franciscans in Europe began to erect sets of Stations in their sanctuaries, and in the early seventeenth century—prompted by the continuing difficulties of pilgrimage to Jerusalem—the pope granted Franciscans official permission for this practice. In 1742 the pope exhorted *all* churches to adorn their sanctuaries with Stations. Around that time, the number of Stations in a set, which had varied from as few as six to as many as thirty, was codified at fourteen, the Stations that are most familiar today. As a result the practice is universal in Catholic congregations, a familiar and much-loved devotion.

The Stations remained rare in Protestant churches, with the exception of highly liturgical Anglican and Lutheran congregations. But in the late twentieth century, as part of a surge of interest in liturgical practices across Reformed and Free Church traditions, individual pastors and churches began to follow the Stations of the Cross. Today it is possible to find Stations in worship—primarily during Holy Week—in Reformed, evangelical, and Baptist churches. Some congregations pare down these Stations to the eight "New Testament" Stations. Many other churches pray the entire traditional fourteen. And the Roman Catholic Church, under the prompting of John Paul II, has developed a cycle of fourteen New Testament Stations, adding to these a fifteenth, depicting the resurrection.

All these forms of the Stations have merit. But the traditional fourteen Stations have a particular spiritual depth and power, perpetuating a long, rich, and significant tradition of biblical commentary that incorporates Old Testament texts to comment on the passion.

Stations III, VII, and IX, which picture Christ falling under the weight of the cross, show us—visually and viscerally—Christ's gradually diminishing energy: he falls, each time, a measure lower. And Station VI, where Christ embraces Mary, offers a poignant mirror image to Station XIII, the Pietà, where Mary embraces the dead body of her son. The Pietà is surely a crucial image, an essential correlative to images of the nativity. For to fully understand the arc of Christ's life, we need to trace his ascent from the manger and Mary's loving arms to his descent into death and her embrace.

Suggestions for Praying the Stations

While retaining the traditional fourteen Stations, this book offers a new worship service of the Stations of the Cross. We have crafted a spare service, allowing time for silent reflection on the visual images as well as for meditation through the simplest means: the biblical texts, a brief prayer, and a chant. We have included a theological reflection for each Station. These may be read aloud as part of corporate worship; they may also be reserved for private study and prayer.

We envision many ways to use this book, imagining many individuals and groups who might find it meaningful and strengthening. We invite readers to envision still more. Among its uses may be to introduce a congregation to the Stations or to offer a fresh entrance into the practice in a parish where long familiarity with the Stations has muted the power of the experience. The book can inform discussions of the passion narrative and encourage our examination of the theological and pastoral significance of the passion in our lives. It can awaken us to the outrage of human suffering and injustice and confirm our resistance to such evil. Praying the Stations may assist the work of small prayer groups or Bible study groups, pastoral care teams, and social justice ministries. In times of sorrow, struggle, or conflict, it may offer comfort and direction to individuals, small groups, or entire congregations. This book may also allow those unable to leave their homes, because of illness or the fragility of age, to attend a Stations service and bear witness. And it is available to any individual as an ongoing spiritual practice.

Praying the Stations of the Cross is a practice that knows no season. The discipline speaks to us powerfully during Lent and Holy Week observances. But it also offers consolation at times of suffering and grief, reassuring us of our great hope as Christians. To that end, this book encourages us to study the Stations; to dwell with Scripture; to pray *with* the images of Christ's passion and *for* the world for which Christ died; to reflect deeply on the meaning of our Lord's incarnation, passion, and resurrection. For the Stations of the Cross are Christ's life, lived and suffered then, alive and urgent now: the narrative of the world's deliverance by cross and by victory.

SECTION II

| | | | | | | | | | | | | | | |

Praying the Stations

A Service of Scripture, Prayer, Image, and Meditation

LET US PRAY:

O Lord God, whose mercy is over all your works, be present in power and great blessing on those who would walk this way of the cross in pilgrimage. As they fall, strengthen them; as they weep with the sorrows of this world, console them; as they bear burdens others thrust upon them, lift them up. You only are high and lofty; you alone eternal; you alone the goodness and life of all the living. Bend down your ear to your creatures' cries. Lift up the lowly, O Lord, and make this earth once again the paradise of your creation, where the leaves of every tree are for the healing of the nations, and where every spring is a river of life. Above all, we pray, make us to know your Son, his passion, and his passionate life. Break open our hearts to be as his, moved with pity, consumed by zeal for righteousness, a prisoner of hope, waiting and searching for the risen life that opens every grave and makes all things new.

All this we ask in the name of the crucified and risen One, Jesus Christ. Amen.

| | | | | | | | | | | | | | | | | | | | | | | | |

STATION I

Jesus Is Condemned to Death

| | | | | | | | | | | | | | | | | | | | | | | | |

STATION I

Jesus Is Condemned to Death

Then Pilate took Jesus and had him flogged. And the soldiers wove a crown of thorns and put it on his head, and they dressed him in a purple robe. They kept coming up to him, saying, "Hail, King of the Jews!" and striking him on the face. Pilate went out again and said to them, "Look, I am bringing him out to you to let you know that I find no case against him." So Jesus came out, wearing the crown of thorns and the purple robe. Pilate said to them, "Here is the man!"

John 19:1–5

Silence is observed

Is it nothing to you, all you who pass by?
Look and see if there is any sorrow like my sorrow.

Lamentations 1:12

PRAYER

Lord Christ, as we meditate on your passion, may we remember
also those for whom you died.
Hear our prayers this day:
for all who are imprisoned, justly or unjustly;
for those who hold others prisoner;
for all those who are tortured or who torture;
for those held prisoner by disease, poverty, famine, or
disaster;
for those bound by fear or loneliness.
We pray also for all those we name now, either aloud or in the
silence of our hearts.

Pause

We gather up these prayers in the name of the One who became
prisoner for our sake, Jesus Christ. Amen.

TAIZÉ CHANT

Stay with me,
remain here with me,
watch and pray,
watch and pray.

MEDITATION

Jesus stands before us, open to our gaze, bound and vulnerable, sorrowful. Even at the end of this long night of interrogation, humiliation, and pain, he reaches out his hands in a gesture of compassion.

But the question posed in Lamentations challenges us all: *Is it nothing to you, all you who pass by? Look and see if there is any sorrow like my sorrow* (Lamentations 1:12). For who among us can stand to witness suffering? Elie Wiesel offers this indictment: "It is so much easier to look away from victims. It is so much easier to avoid such rude interruptions to our work, our dreams, our hopes." How true that each of us is far more likely to avert our eyes, to pass by on the other side. We are far more likely to be among those who on that day—and on every day—pass by the "place of the skull," the Roman wasteland set aside for crucifixion. Albert Schweitzer enjoined us to "think occasionally of the suffering of which we spare ourselves the sight." Yet we walk past. We carry on our lives completely self-absorbed and indifferent to the three crosses pitted against the dark sky. We participate in the abandonment of Christ.

And the abandonment of Christ is reenacted—in every nation and in every age—whenever suffering is met with callous isolation and blindness. This is what we mean when we say that Christ is crucified wherever the poor and powerless are suffering and abandoned. This does not mean that Christ dies in every age or that the poor and oppressed are themselves a second Christ. But because of the death of Jesus Christ, the sin of abandonment is known for what it is: the willingness of humankind to ignore suffering so that our own lives are pursued conveniently and without interruption. This seemingly benign neglect is exposed as rebellion against God.

But over against this universal human inclination, Christ offers the structure of compassion. When asked to summarize the Law, Jesus answers, *"You shall love the Lord your God with all your heart, and with all your soul, and with all your mind, and with all your strength."* After this first commandment he gives the second: *"You shall love your neighbor as yourself." There is no commandment greater than these* (Mark 12:30–31). Jesus teaches here that our love of self—our intense preoccupation with our own lives, our single-minded pursuit of our own ends, our effortless defense of our own way of seeing things—is also to be accorded to our neighbor. He affirms that our willingness to imagine the joys and suffering of our neighbors *as though they were our own* is indeed the proper worship of God.

Let us pray for the strength to turn aside from our preoccupations, to see truly, to acknowledge in heart and mind the suffering that Christ undertook for our sake, and—through that awareness of Christ's suffering—to look on the sorrows of the world.

STATION II

Jesus Takes Up His Cross

Jesus Takes Up His Cross

READINGS FROM SCRIPTURE

Then [Pilate] handed [Jesus] over to [the Jewish leaders] to be crucified. So they took Jesus; and carrying the cross by himself, he went
out to what is called The Place of the Skull, which in Hebrew is called
Golgotha.

John 19:16–17

Silence is observed

"Let us lie in wait for the righteous man,
because he is inconvenient to us and opposes our actions;
he reproaches us for sins against the law,
and accuses us of sins against our training.
He professes to have knowledge of God,
and calls himself a child of the Lord.
He became to us a reproof of our thoughts;
the very sight of him is a burden to us,
because his manner of life is unlike that of others,
and his ways are strange.
We are considered by him as something base,
and he avoids our ways as unclean;
he calls the last end of the righteous happy,
and boasts that God is his father.
Let us see if his words are true,

and let us test what will happen at the end of his life;
for if the righteous man is God's child, he will help him,
and will deliver him from the hand of his adversaries.
Let us test him with insult and torture,
so that we may find out how gentle he is,
and make trial of his forbearance.
Let us condemn him to a shameful death,
for, according to what he says, he will be protected."

Wisdom 2:12–20

PRAYER

Lord Christ, as we meditate on your passion, may we remember
also those for whom you died.
Hear our prayers this day:
for all who carry heavy burdens;
for those weighed down by fear;
for those living with pain, disease, or long illness;
for those caring for the sick;
for those keeping watch over the dying;
for those homeless who must bear their possessions on their
backs.
We pray also for all those we name either aloud or in the silence of
our hearts.

Pause

We gather up these prayers in the name of the One who bore us
and our sins to the grave, Jesus Christ. Amen.

TAIZÉ CHANT

Stay with me,
remain here with me,
watch and pray,
watch and pray.

MEDITATION

Jesus begins here his downward journey: down from Pilate's lofty palace, down from the courtyard and praetorium, down the Via Dolorosa, and down—over and over again—on his knees, under the weight of the cross. Christ and the cross fill the space as he lifts that burden, steadying its cruel weight with shoulders, head, hands. His whole body is bent beneath this load, the cross that is his death, the cross that is freighted with the groaning weight of the world's sin, and weighted as well with betrayal.

It is so ingrained in us that Jesus enters into his passion through the act of betrayal that we scarcely stop to examine this brute and brutal fact: Jesus is betrayed by one of his followers, by one of his intimates, by one of us. What does this mean, for us and for our salvation? What does holy Scripture seek to teach us about Christ's death when it insists, in every mention of Judas Iscariot, that he is a *traitor*, but also reminds us that each disciple, when challenged by Jesus's words, *One of you will betray me*, responds, *Surely not I, Lord?* And even Judas himself, in Matthew's Gospel, asks, when handed the sop of bread, *Surely not I, Rabbi?* (Matthew 26:21–25). We are confronted here by the deeply private character of betrayal, an act so hidden from our eyes and our hearts that Christ's followers—including we ourselves—do not know if we might be that very traitor.

In Christ's saving death there is the public character of arrest and beating and contempt and execution. But there is also this secret aspect to his death. For Jesus Christ seeks to save us in the external, the public, the visible elements of our lives and our culture, and he seeks also—and indeed accomplishes—the salvation of our secret, inward, and most hidden selves. Jesus Christ enters into our dearest relationships, our private lives; he is the Savior not only in the midst of the love but also in the face of the cruelty and indifference and betrayal that compose our earthly families and friendships. We need not bring him into a broken partnership, into a ruined friendship, into a lost and cold family: Jesus is *there*, already there, strong to save. Even within his own disciples, as he takes his place at the table, distrust and fear and calculation have entered the circle of the Twelve. But the gospel tells us that Jesus Christ is the Savior of all such betrayals, the faithful One in the midst of all such treason.

But the gospel reaches even further than that! For holy Scripture shows us that Christ is the Physician of our own inner lives, of our very selves, even of those betrayals that lie hidden from our eyes. Jesus sees already the conflict that lies at the heart of each disciple, each follower and friend. Long before we are disclosed to ourselves as the mistaken, sometimes venal, so often foolish followers of our Lord, Christ has seen and known and loved us. He knows our betrayal of his causes; he knows our longing to name someone else as traitor; he knows that we cannot be sure of ourselves. He knows our deepest questions: *Surely not I, Lord? Will I betray? Will I flee? Will I deny my Lord three times?*

And the answer Jesus gives is this: that he is content to be betrayed and handed over to sinners; he is content to be surrounded by disciples such as we are; he is content to sit at table with us and to walk to his end in our company. He is content to be our Savior. This is what it means for him to look upon our hearts, as he did on the hearts of Nathaniel and Nicodemus, Mary and Martha and the woman at the well, and Judas Iscariot, so many years ago in Israel. This is what it means for Jesus to be glorified as the Lamb of God who takes away the sin of the world, the sin of every faithless and traitorous heart. To this gospel of faithful and suffering love, we can only reply: "Thanks be to God!"

| | | | | | | | | | | | | | | | | | | | | | | |

STATION III

Jesus Falls the First Time

| | | | | | | | | | | | | | | | | | | | | | |

Jesus Falls the First Time

READINGS FROM SCRIPTURE

Then [Jesus] began to teach them that the Son of Man must undergo great suffering, and be rejected by the elders, the chief priests, and the scribes, and be killed, and after three days rise again.... He called the crowd with his disciples, and said to them, "If any want to become my followers, let them deny themselves and take up their cross and follow me. For those who want to save their life will lose it, and those who lose their life for my sake, and for the sake of the gospel, will save it."

Mark 8:31, 34–35

Silence is observed

By a perversion of justice he was taken away.
    Who could have imagined his future?
For he was cut off from the land of the living,
    stricken for the transgression of my people.
They made his grave with the wicked
    and his tomb with the rich,

although he had done no violence,
    and there was no deceit in his mouth.

Isaiah 53:8–9

PRAYER

Lord Christ, as we meditate on your passion, may we remember
    also those for whom you died.
Hear our prayers this day:
    for all whose tasks and sorrows are beyond what they can
        bear;
    for those carrying the burden of illness;
    for those fallen beneath the weight of poverty or
        homelessness;
    for those stricken by shame, guilt, or fear;
    for those suffering from violence, oppression, or degradation.
We pray also for all those we name either aloud or in the silence of
    our hearts.

Pause

We gather up these prayers in the name of the One who falls under the cross of sorrow, Jesus Christ. Amen.

TAIZÉ CHANT

Stay with me,
remain here with me,
watch and pray,
watch and pray.

MEDITATION

We watch as Jesus staggers, falls under the weight of the cross. He braces himself against the massive beam, steadying his body on the wood and relying on its weight to support his own. His hands tear on the rough-hewn logs; his brow bleeds from the thorns. We feel the dead weight of this instrument of execution, a weapon that crushes its victims even as they carry it to the place of death, this cross that is so specifically the Roman form of execution.

Crucifixion summed up, with a particular and searing form of ferocity, the relation between Rome, the reigning "great power" of its day, and those subjugated peoples who did not submit with gratitude to the mercies of the Pax Romana. It was a slave's death, reserved for all who were not Roman citizens, a means of capital punishment wielded as a threat, a torture designed to terrify and control the people who witnessed it.

For crucifixion was not a quick and efficient form of execution, but rather one that—by its very design—inflicted suffering and humiliation, both in secret and in the public gaze. The enemy of the state was held in a dark prison, where the contempt and shaming of the victim could begin, unseen and unchecked. A human being, a living creature of God, became an *object*, a plaything of great powers. Mocked and humiliated, beaten and whipped, he was forced to carry his cross to the place of death. Then, hung by his own flesh, his arms suspended from a crossbeam, his feet nailed into a beam dug into the blood-soaked earth, the crucified victim was exposed in every way. Stripped, bleeding, and raw, naked to the avid gaze of spectators, open to taunting and contempt, he died slowly of his own weight, starving for breath, for water, for pity.

And the point of these secret and then public torments, as with so many modern forms of torture, was to allow the victim to live. Death was the release, not the penalty. And on this Roman tree of cruelty hung the Son of Man for the deliverance of the world. Christ's death is the execution of the *"King of the Jews"* by the Roman imperial state. Branded as the King who would rival Caesar, he is raised up on the cross, crucified in this particular imperial torment. The royal claimant, he is executed by the death reserved for the alien, the off-scouring of empire, the slave.

Paul, in his great hymn to the incarnation in Philippians, tells us that Christ did not exploit his equality with God *but emptied himself, taking the form of a slave* (Philippians 2:6–7). And Jesus becomes a possession (surely the most basic and defining element of slavery), the property of the state, the subject and plaything of an empire that sweeps its slaves away as so much trash, as offending foreigners who disturb the peace of royal palaces.

But this death reaches far beyond, offers us far more than an instance of the dehumanizing power of empire. For Jesus, by the cross, by its public scandal and shame and offense, takes on—becomes—the curse that properly belongs to us all, to the rebel subjects of God. In the death of this one slave, the world's sin becomes the possession and vestment of the sinless One, who takes on, assumes, and bears our rebellion against God. In Christ's death we see the depth of a wondrous exchange. Christ annihilates radically, and finally unmakes, the sin of empires and also of rebels. To redeem the sinful world, the Word and Lord of life becomes the curse that is the very rebellion against him and his reign; and in his death under the form of a slave, he uncreates and annihilates our sin. Through death he conquers death.

||||||||||||||||||||||||

STATION IV

Jesus Meets His Grieving Mother

||||||||||||||||||||||||

Jesus Meets His Grieving Mother

READINGS FROM SCRIPTURE

What can I say for you, to what compare you,
    O daughter Jerusalem?
To what can I liken you, that I may comfort you,
    O virgin daughter Zion?
For vast as the sea is your ruin;
    Who can heal you?

Lamentations 2:13

Silence is observed

"Call me no longer Naomi,
    call me Mara,
    for the Almighty has dealt bitterly with me.
I went away full,
    but the LORD has brought me back empty."

Ruth 1:20–21a

PRAYER

Lord Christ, as we meditate on your passion, may we remember
also those for whom you died.
Hear our prayers this day:
for all who witness the suffering of those they love;
for all those who watch beside a sickbed;
for all those who keep vigil with the dying;
for those who fear for a missing or wounded child;
for those who grieve for a loved one in danger.
We pray also for all those we name either aloud or in the silence of
our hearts.

Pause

We gather up these prayers in the name of the One who grew
and became strong in his mother's loving care, Jesus Christ.
Amen.

TAIZÉ CHANT

Stay with me,
remain here with me,
watch and pray,
watch and pray.

MEDITATION

How often has the church portrayed Mary with every sign of glory and splendor: covered in yards of cloth of gold, seated on thrones or brocaded cushions, crowned with a golden circlet that outshines the heavens, honored with titles that exalt her as Queen of Heaven, Star of the Sea. All these are markers of Mary's unscaled heights as the Theotokos, the God-bearer.

But this Mary is different: a distraught and grieving mother, she is cradled and comforted in the arms of the son who has been beaten and scorned and finally condemned to die a painful and humiliating death. We know this Mary from the evening news; she is the woman whose son is among those "disappeared" into a system of repression and torture. We know her as our neighbor, whose child is diagnosed with cancer. She is a sister—or a brother—whose dearest friend is caught in a fiery car crash. She is any of us. And she reminds us that our human life is knit up most intimately with the life of the Son of God, as his is in ours.

We might call this Mary, with the greatest possible honor, Mary the humble one, Mary the lowly. And we might remember what we have learned of Mary from her song, the Magnificat, where Mary speaks of herself as the lowly, the handmaid, the humble. How easy it has been for the church to confound this title, the humble one, with subservience, so that we have understood Mary—even in the midst of the great glories assigned to her—as Mary the meek, the submissive, the mild. But holy Scripture does not allow us to make such an easy mistake. For the Greek term used for Mary's lowliness is not just any term, any marker of poverty and weakness, but is rather the very word St. Paul uses to describe the mind of Christ. In the Christ hymn in Philippians 2, it is Christ himself, the One fully equal to God, who empties himself, and finding himself in human form, humbles himself, becoming like Mary, and she like him, the true lowly ones of the earth.

God's glory, we learn here, is to be lowly. God, the true Lord of all the earth, is not only the majestic One, shrouded in awe and mystery. It is his very majesty and nature to be humble. And we who are granted grace to follow him, to seek after him, are freed to follow him as did Mary: to stand among the last and least, to join their ranks, to become the bruised reed, and to bind up the brokenhearted; to follow Mary to her Son's cross, and to stand under that cross, between broken thieves. This is the glory of the Christian life, the glory of Mary, and, above all, the glory of God himself, the One who is perfected in weakness.

STATION V

The Cross Is Laid on Simon of Cyrene

The Cross Is Laid on Simon of Cyrene

READINGS FROM SCRIPTURE

As they led [Jesus] away, they seized a man, Simon of Cyrene, who was coming from the country, and they laid the cross on him, and made him carry it behind Jesus.

Luke 23:26

Silence is observed

Surely he has borne our infirmities
    and carried our diseases;
yet we accounted him stricken,
    struck down by God, and afflicted.
But he was wounded for our transgressions,
    crushed for our iniquities;
upon him was the punishment that made us whole,
    and by his bruises we are healed.

Isaiah 53:4–5

PRAYER

Lord Christ, as we meditate on your passion, may we remember
also those for whom you died.

Hear our prayers this day:

for those who carry our burdens;

for those who stand beside us in times of sickness and
danger;

for those who shield us from harm;

for those whose love supports and carries us across dark
places;

for those whose hands prepare for us food and warmth and
shelter;

for ourselves, that we may have the grace to allow others to
assist us.

We pray also for all those we name either aloud or in the silence of
our hearts.

Pause

We gather up these prayers in the name of the One who stands in
our place and shoulders our burdens, Jesus Christ. Amen.

TAIZÉ CHANT

Stay with me,
remain here with me,
watch and pray,
watch and pray.

MEDITATION

Simon of Cyrene is an unwilling actor in the events of the passion. Matthew and Mark write that he was *compelled*, and Luke tells us that Simon was *seized* and *made* to carry the cross for Jesus. But who would take on this task willingly? Who would step forth from the crowd—even knowing that this cross is for another's death—to carry this load amid the heat, and the dust, and the jeering of the crowd? Who among us would take this on for another?

This question casts in high relief the willingness of the One who has given over this load to another for this short journey only, but who has also—for all eternity—taken on the burden of our sins and even death itself, for our sake. Christ declares in John's Gospel: *I am the good shepherd. The good shepherd lays down his life for his sheep. . . . I know my own, and my own know me* (John 10:11, 14). It would be hard to find a saying more familiar, or more comforting, to Christians that this one.

But Christ continues: *The hired hand, who is not the shepherd and does not own the sheep, sees the wolf coming and leaves the sheep and runs away—and the wolf snatches them and scatters them* (John 10:12). And we wonder about this minor character, the hired man, this shadow figure who stands off to one side, a character in someone else's drama. As with Simon, we know almost nothing about him. As with Simon, the hired man also does not willingly take on this burden, will not lay down his life. The sheep do not know him or his voice; they are not led into his fold or protected by his staff.

The hireling abandons the sheep, Scripture tells us, because he does not own them. Do we not know this failure well? Can we forget the disciples who fled from their Lord? And Peter—the chief hireling—who denied his Shepherd three times? Are we not disciples just like these? Do we not know the lot of this hired hand and of Simon himself, their failures and facelessness?

66

For just that reason we must lift our eyes from the hireling to the shepherd, move our focus from the shadows to the great Light. For it is Christ's vocation—his alone—to be the good shepherd whose life saves and defends the lost sheep. To his voice alone we listen, and to him we are neither hired nor coerced labor. We are not owned or hired or compelled by him, but we *are* his own. He knows us; and in his turning toward us, we know him. He alone is the true shepherd, the ransomer of all the disciples who saw the wolf and fled, of all those who only unwillingly take on the sorrows and burdens of others.

For in him the hireling, the unwilling servant, is not abandoned or forgotten. Because—and this is the astonishing grace of Scripture—the true, good, and perfect hired hand is this one Jesus of Nazareth. Is he not the very One who took his place among the faceless and lost, who was rejected and scorned? Is he not the true stranger in our midst, whose face is disguised in the poor and lost of every age? Is he not the One, in his life and in his death, who enters into the land of the lost, the failed, and the forgotten, to lead us out into his own good pasture?

Yes, Jesus Christ is the good shepherd and the true hireling, the bearer of all burdens. He lays down his life for his own. And this is the great and good news. It is the reason, the basis, and the hope of all our ministries. It is the grace in which we all stand. Thanks be to God.

STATION VI

A Woman Wipes the Face of Jesus

A Woman Wipes the Face of Jesus

READINGS FROM SCRIPTURE

> My eyes flow with rivers of tears
>> because of the destruction of my people.
> My eyes will flow without ceasing,
>> without respite,
> until the LORD from heaven
>> looks down and sees.
> My eyes cause me grief
>> at the fate of all the young women in my city.
>
> Lamentations 3:48–51

Silence is observed

> On this mountain the LORD of hosts will make for all peoples
>> a feast of rich food, a feast of well-aged wines,
>> of rich food filled with marrow, of well-aged wines strained
>>> clear.
> And he will destroy on this mountain
>> the shroud that is cast over all peoples,
>> the sheet that is spread over all nations;
>> he will swallow up death forever.

71

Then the Lord GOD will wipe away the tears from all faces,
>   and the disgrace of his people he will take away from all
>   the earth,
>   for the LORD has spoken.
It will be said on that day,
>   Lo, this is our God; we have waited for him, so that he might
>   save us.
>   This is the LORD for whom we have waited;
>   let us be glad and rejoice in his salvation.

Isaiah 25:6–9

PRAYER

> Lord Christ, as we meditate on your passion, may we remember
>   also those for whom you died.
> Hear our prayers this day:
>   for all who comfort the suffering;
>   for those who minister to the sick and dying;
>   for those who accept the help we offer;
>   for those who support the unlovely and the unloved;
>   for those who go into dark places to bring them light;
>   for those who know in us the goodness and beauty
>   we do not see.
> We pray also for all those we name either aloud or in the silence of
>   our hearts.

Pause

> We gather up these prayers in the name of the One who is comfort
>   in sorrow and life out of every grave, Jesus Christ. Amen.

TAIZÉ CHANT

> Stay with me,
> remain here with me,
> watch and pray,
> watch and pray.

MEDITATION

She has stepped forward from the crowd to wipe Christ's bleeding brow. Tradition has named her Veronica, after the "true image" (the *vera ikon*), Christ's visage imprinted on her cloth. Perhaps it is a gift that we do not know her name: in this way she stands for each and all of us. And we long to know what compels her to this action, just as we ponder the impact of this meeting. Has she been, day by day, a follower of Jesus? Is she a bystander whose heart is suddenly touched? Does she recognize from long aware-ness—or only now, as she touches him—that she is encountering the Holy One of God? The image of his face is pressed not just into the cloth but onto her heart, as she acknowledges, with solemn pity but with awe as well, the power of this meeting. And so we ask—each of us—what has drawn us to encounter the Holy One of God, and what is the nature of this encounter?

Each of us has been brought here by the call of Jesus of Nazareth. We are all sorts and conditions of people, and we have come by way of the many and varied instruments through which the Lord God has been pleased to call us into his service. We come, perhaps, because we were borne in our mothers' and fathers' arms into the church, one day long ago, to become children of God and members of his people. Or we come because a teacher, or a friend, or a nameless radio evangelist, speaking to us in the dark quiet of a lonely ride, called us to become disciples of this sovereign Lord. Or perhaps, more starkly, we heard Christ's call through the fear, the sorrow, the sheer physicality of illness and pain. Or, more joyfully, we heard this call to discipleship through the solemn beauty of this universe, each part and all parts of which sing the glory of the one Lord. We come for all these reasons and through all these ministers of God's word, and for many more that only we know in our hearts. But we are here, disciples of this one teacher.

Some of us find this encounter, this life of discipleship, is one of deep joy, of delight in knowing whose we are, and for whom we are made, and whose name we serve. This is the peace the Lord gives us, a peace that the world cannot give. But we do not enter very far into our calling, nor into the service and ministry of this particular and gracious Lord, without hearing the danger of this calling, the danger of this encounter with the holiness of this anointed One of Israel. We recall the man with the unclean spirit who, Mark tells us, encounters Jesus in the synagogue at Capernaum. He cries out: *What have you to do with us, Jesus of Nazareth? Have you come to destroy us? I know who you are, the Holy One of God* (Mark 1:24). How significant that the man, and the demons who possess him, recognize the One before whom they stand. And this Jesus has power over the unclean spirits, casting them forth and allowing the sufferer to go free.

But this deliverer and healer, this Holy One of God, is himself the afflicted One. He is himself the One broken on God, the obedient One who went that long way to his death, his abandonment, his unmaking in that tomb outside the city wall. Though he knew no sin, yet he became sin, and in just that way this One became the many, our many. As those who are called to him, we also will stand under his consuming fire—but not alone! For the gospel is this: he has gone this way before. We who follow walk in his path, and our end is not dereliction but great joy. And just like this nameless woman who wipes the face of Jesus, so we too will meet our Savior face-to-face and imprint his visage in our hearts: the Holy One of God, the afflicted deliverer, our gracious Lord and helper.

|||||||||||||||||||||||

STATION VII

Jesus Falls a Second Time

|||||||||||||||||||||

STATION VII

Jesus Falls a Second Time

READINGS FROM SCRIPTURE

Yet it was the will of the LORD to crush him with pain.
When you make his life an offering for sin,
 he shall see his offspring, and shall prolong his days;
through him the will of the LORD shall prosper.
 Out of his anguish he shall see light;
he shall find satisfaction through his knowledge.
 The righteous one, my servant, shall make many righteous,
 and he shall bear their iniquities.
Therefore I will allot him a portion with the great,
 and he shall divide the spoil with the strong;
because he poured out himself to death,
 and was numbered with the transgressors;
yet he bore the sin of many,
 and made intercession for the transgressors.

Isaiah 53:10–12

Silence is observed

I am the scorn of all my adversaries,
 a horror to my neighbors,

an object of dread to my acquaintances;
    those who see me in the street flee from me.
I have passed out of mind like one who is dead;
    I have become like a broken vessel.

Psalm 31:11–12

PRAYER

Lord Christ, as we meditate on your passion, may we remember
    also those for whom you died.
Hear our prayers this day:
    for all those stricken and afflicted;
    for those who have fallen over and again;
    for those felled by pain and illness;
    for those struggling with addiction;
    for those immobilized by fear;
    for those who struggle to stand upright beneath
        their burdens.
We pray also for all those we name either aloud or in the silence of
    our hearts.

Pause

We gather up these prayers in the name of the One who knew
    weakness and affliction and yet gave to us life, Jesus Christ.
    Amen.

TAIZÉ CHANT

Stay with me,
remain here with me,
watch and pray,
watch and pray.

MEDITATION

He falls a second time, forced to his knees, his hands in the dust, his head lowered almost to the ground. Not yet to the end of this cruel journey, he is exhausted from the long night of interrogation, humiliation, and pain. This righteous One of God, the Son of Man, has been bound, abused, and beaten; placed on exhibit by the soldiers and guards of imperial Rome; mocked for the sport of it. And now he struggles even to stand, exposed not just to the broiling sun but also to the scorn and rejection of the crowds, avid for blood, eager for the suffering to come.

As Christians we are enjoined to see Christ in all prisoners and captives, those who are poor, unloved, unwanted. Christ's identification, his very intimacy with all those who are tortured, humiliated, and abused, is so burned into our hearts and minds that when Christians face the terrible fact of prisoner torture and abuse—in our own day as in every age—we find set before us the image of Jesus. And we understand that Jesus Christ is sinned against in every cruelty visited against any captive.

The torture and humiliation of prisoners does not begin with the abuse of Jesus of Nazareth. We know that the practice of abuse is universal and ageless. We recognize that torture—assault on human dignity—belongs to every age. It is as ancient as the Servant Songs of Isaiah, lamenting the torment of ancient Israel. Indeed the horror and desecration of God's creatures is as old as Abel's blood crying out from the ground and Tamar's despair at the violence from her brother Amnon's hand.

It may seem to us, however, as though torture and abuse are horrors before God only when carried out against the innocent, most especially against the unique and sinless innocence of the Son of God. We may imagine that humiliation and cruelty do not violate our faith when wielded against the dangerous or the guilty. We may convince ourselves that times of war, or threats to our security, or the need for retribution can serve to mitigate torture, that such acts are justified if they do not violate the innocent.

But any and all torture is an act *against God*, a rebellion against God, because it acts against God's very goodness, compassion, and fidelity. For God takes frail sinners as his very own, to be the fruit of his own redeeming. That all human creatures are sinners is a maxim of both Testaments of the Christian Bible: Israel has abandoned the widow and the orphan; and Peter and Judas have betrayed the Lord they loved; and all of us have gone astray like lost sheep. But the joyous message of both Testaments is that God is the hope and preservation of these very sinners. God's gracious covenant rises out of the everlasting mercy and kindness of God and is renewed day by day, every day.

To mock, to scorn, to abuse and torment these creatures, beloved of God, redeemed by his suffering and his outstretched arm, is to mock God and his loving-kindness. Those who tortured our Lord did this once, long ago, as did all those who stood as witnesses to the crucifixion. May we Christians, sinners all, repent of these acts and learn of them no more.

STATION VIII

Jesus Meets the Women of Jerusalem

Jesus Meets the Women of Jerusalem

READINGS FROM SCRIPTURE

A great number of the people followed him, and among them were women who were beating their breasts and wailing for him. But Jesus turned to them and said, "Daughters of Jerusalem, do not weep for me, but weep for yourselves and for your children. For the days are surely coming when they will say, 'Blessed are the barren, and the wombs that never bore, and the breasts that never nursed.' Then they will begin to say to the mountains, 'Fall on us'; and to the hills, 'Cover us.' For if they do this when the wood is green, what will happen when it is dry?"

Luke 23:27–31

Silence is observed

The elders of daughter Zion
    sit on the ground in silence;
they have thrown dust on their heads
    and put on sackcloth;
the young girls of Jerusalem
    have bowed their heads to the ground.

Lamentations 2:10

PRAYER

Lord Christ, as we meditate on your passion, may we remember
also those for whom you died.
Hear our prayers this day:
for all who face darkness in their lives;
for those who fear for themselves and their future;
for those grief-stricken for their children and grandchildren;
for those who live in times of war and strife;
for those who live in places of famine or disaster.
We pray also for all those we name either aloud or in the silence of
our hearts.

Pause

We gather up these prayers in the name of the One who tasted
sorrow for our sake, Jesus Christ. Amen.

TAIZÉ CHANT

Stay with me,
remain here with me,
watch and pray,
watch and pray.

MEDITATION

The women who have followed Jesus through town and countryside, sitting at his feet, gathering their children under his gaze, now stand appalled, wailing at his countenance—so marred and disfigured—and in dreadful anticipation of the slow and agonizing death to come. But he charges them to weep, not for him, but rather for themselves. And then follow words of dire prophecy: *For the days are surely coming when they will say, "Blessed are the barren, and the wombs that never bore, and the breasts that never nursed"* (Luke 23:29).

What is this word of woe, this message of darkness? We ordinarily think of almighty God and his word, revealed in holy Scripture, as the source of light and not of darkness, of peace, redemption, and weal, and not of woe. And yet one of the lessons of our adulthood as Christians is the reality, perhaps even the inevitability, of darkness and woe in our own lives and in the lives of the nations of the world.

Yet often the darkness and woe cannot be expressed. What words can capture the loss of our work or our home, of our good name, of our joy and satisfaction in life? What does it mean for us to suffer pain; to lose someone we love; to suffer disappointment in ourselves; to examine our lives before God and taste the bitterness of failing to love God and neighbor above self; to understand our faith in God sorely tried, sometimes shattered, by these shadows that have fallen across our lives? We know—if only in sighs too deep for words—what it means to have darkness and woe enter our lives.

This is what theologian Karl Barth called the "shadow side" of life: not evil, yet standing near to it, reminding us that for every morning there is evening; for every light, darkness; for every seedtime, harvest and the end. Scripture affirms that even such "alien work" belongs to God. *I form light and create darkness, I make weal and create woe; I the LORD do all these things* (Isaiah 45:7). What should we make of the shadow side of our lives, of the enigmatic dark lines in the lives of the peoples of the earth?

We believe that even in these works of his "left hand" God is at work, that they also are under his guidance, providence, and redemption. We must seek in prayer, in study, and in life together to discern what God's will may be for us in such works. For these are a testing and school for us all. We do not read off the answers for these problems like so many simple sums. Rather, we must seek to enter each day more deeply into the surpassing mystery that is God, into the hidden mystery that is God in Christ. When we look toward Christ's life, we see the grace that breaks out from obedience, suffering, and death. We see the shadow side of darkness and woe turned toward the light. We see Christ's death putting death to flight. For we are instructed, loved, and fed at the hand of One who tasted the bitter cup to the end, who knows our lot, who takes us for his own. In the life and death of Jesus Christ, we can see the one true and dazzling place where God has said: *I form light and create darkness, I make weal and create woe; I the* LORD *do all these things.*

STATION IX

Jesus Falls a Third Time

Jesus Falls a Third Time

READINGS FROM SCRIPTURE

> Then deep from the earth you shall speak,
>> from low in the dust your words shall come;
> your voice shall come from the ground like the voice of a ghost,
>> and your speech shall whisper out of the dust.
>
> Isaiah 29:4

Silence is observed

> He was oppressed, and he was afflicted,
>> yet he did not open his mouth;
> like a lamb that is led to the slaughter,
>> and like a sheep that before its shearers is silent,
>> so he did not open his mouth.
>
> Isaiah 53:7

PRAYER

> Lord Christ, as we meditate on your passion, may we remember
>> also those for whom you died.
> Hear our prayers this day:
>> for all those who are brought low;
>> for those imprisoned by despair;
>> for those with no hope for recovery or healing;
>> for those ground down by poverty, fear, or illness;
>> for those who are wounded by oppression, violence,
>>> or degradation.
> We pray also for all those we name either aloud or in the silence of
>> our hearts.

Pause

> We gather up these prayers in the name of the One who went
>> down to the dust that we might be exalted, Jesus Christ.
>> Amen.

TAIZÉ CHANT

> Stay with me,
> remain here with me,
> watch and pray,
> watch and pray.

MEDITATION

This time, the third time, Jesus falls to the ground. Worn from the long night of interrogation and torture, exhausted by the journey to the place of death, he still summons the strength to lift his head. His blood, from thorn and lash and rope, mingles with the dust. And we are reminded of that first blood shed—that primal act of violence, brother against brother—and of God's cry to Cain: *What have you done?*

And when Cain replies, in words that we so often echo in our words or live out through our actions, *Am I my brother's keeper?*, God calls out in judgment, *Listen, your brother's blood is crying out to me from the ground! And now you are cursed from the ground, which has opened its mouth to receive your brother's blood from your hand* (Genesis 4:9–11).

So the blood that is spilled out onto the ground by Cain's hands, by our own hands, does not remain silent. It enters into the creation itself, the "mouth" of the earth. And out of that mouth the blood—of our brother, sister, neighbor, friend, enemy—cries out. And the Almighty commands us to listen to that voice. But all of us, children of Adam and Eve, have grown deaf to that voice: over the centuries so much blood has spilled into the sea and the earth, and it cries out so loud that we cannot hear it. Murder and warfare spill that blood. But so too, Christ tells us, does a moment's anger or an easy word of contempt. The denying of water to the little ones, the passing by on the other side of those left for dead, the act of loving while counting the cost, the hatred of enemies— all these carry the mark of Cain, a brother's blood spilled into the earth. And we are commanded to turn our deaf ears to that incarnadine earth, to listen to that voice.

God calls us to open our ears, to hear the blood of Abel, the brother whose sacrifice was pleasing to God and thus incited Cain's murderous wrath. But while we all share in Cain's sin, we no longer fall under Cain's indictment. For we have as our guide and salvation the voice of the true and pleasing sacrifice, the true keeper of the sheep, the One whose blood, poured out onto the earth, is our own health and hope. Christ's blood does not condemn us but rather frees us. He is the true Abel. And when he rides in triumph into his royal city, and the Pharisees demand: *Teacher, order your disciples to stop*, he answers: *I tell you, if these were silent, the stones would shout out* (Luke 19:39–40).

Listen! The blood of our brother cries out from the earth! Do we hear it?

STATION X

Jesus Is Stripped of His Garments

Jesus Is Stripped of His Garments

READINGS FROM SCRIPTURE

When the soldiers had crucified Jesus, they took his clothes and divided them into four parts, one for each soldier. They also took his tunic; now the tunic was seamless, woven in one piece from the top. So they said to one another, "Let us not tear it, but cast lots for it to see who will get it." This was to fulfill what the scripture says,

"They divided my clothes among themselves,
and for my clothing they cast lots."

And that is what the soldiers did.

John 19:23–25

Silence is observed

Then Job arose, tore his robe, shaved his head, and fell on the ground and worshiped. He said, "Naked I came from my mother's womb, and naked shall I return there; the LORD gave, and the LORD has taken away; blessed be the name of the LORD."

Job 1:20–21

PRAYER

Lord Christ, as we meditate on your passion, may we remember
   also those for whom you died.
Hear our prayers this day:
   For all those who are stripped and exposed;
   for those who have lost their homes and possessions;
   for those who are shorn of their name and reputation;
   for those whose sense of their own worth has been taken
      from them;
   for those without health, or home, or companionship.
We pray also for all those we name either aloud or in the silence of
   our hearts.

Pause

We gather up these prayers in the name of the One who emptied
   himself and took the name of a slave, our Savior Jesus Christ.
   Amen.

TAIZÉ CHANT

Stay with me,
remain here with me,
watch and pray,
watch and pray.

MEDITATION

Here, at the end of this terrible journey, Jesus is stripped of his garments. Beaten and bleeding, exhausted, alone, the Son of God is now naked, defenseless, exposed to the gaze—the ridicule and contempt—of the authorities, the soldiers, the crowd. By a cruel irony, the King of Angels is abandoned, homeless, with barely a rag to cover his nakedness.

And how are we to think of this—those of us in a society so full of possessions? Are we not like the rich young man (Luke calls him the rich ruler) who, asking Jesus what he must do to inherit the kingdom of heaven, receives the answer, *Go, sell your possessions, and give the money to the poor, and you will have treasure in heaven; then come, follow me.* And the young man *went away grieving, for he had many possessions* (Matthew 19:21–22).

The challenge that Jesus metes out to the rich young man stands before us too. We might say before us especially. For we are the comfortable of the earth, our country the wealthiest and most powerful among the family of nations. When we hear this story, as when we see our Lord stripped and abandoned, do we not also experience the sadness of the rich young man, the sting and shame of disciples who, unlike their master, cover themselves in fine raiment and sit in ivory palaces?

But the story of the rich young man, our story, is never just a tale about greed or complacency or fear. Jesus's commandment is not just a commandment about things. The story is always about the call to him, to Jesus. And *he* is the man of sorrows, the One acquainted with grief.

To have to do with him, with Jesus Christ, is to glimpse the shattering truth of his dispossession, of his trial, of his grief. And this truth—of the way of the cross—fills the rich young man, his disciples, and us with anguish. But marvelously, graciously, Jesus bears even that sorrow to his crucifixion. On his cross Jesus takes for his very own the fear and anguish, the poverty and lack that every disciple exhibits. Though the rich young man abandons Jesus, Jesus does not forsake him, or us. The cross of Christ is for the rich young man and for us, in our possessions and in our poverty. In our disobedience, fear, and greed, Jesus commands and calls us but also delivers us.

May we this day truly hear his word and follow where he leads. May the Lord grant us grace to turn from our disobedience into his faithfulness, from our possessions into his dispossession, from our death into his life. May this way of the cross become to us the very way of life and health and treasure in heaven.

STATION XI

Jesus Is Nailed to the Cross

Jesus Is Nailed to the Cross

READINGS FROM SCRIPTURE

When they came to the place that is called The Skull, they crucified
Jesus there with the criminals, one on his right and one on his left.

Luke 23:33

Silence is observed

Abraham took the wood of the burnt offering and laid it on his son
Isaac, and he himself carried the fire and the knife. So the two of
them walked on together. Isaac said to his father Abraham, "Father!"
And he said, "Here I am, my son." He said, "The fire and the wood
are here, but where is the lamb for a burnt offering?" Abraham said,
"God himself will provide the lamb for a burnt offering, my son." So
the two of them walked on together.

Genesis 22:6–8

PRAYER

Lord Christ, as we meditate on your passion, may we remember
also those for whom you died.
Hear our prayers this day:
for all those who are pierced by fear;
for those scourged by poverty or disease;
for those transfixed by anger, hatred, or self-loathing;
for those held hostage by oppression or prejudice.
We pray also for all those we name either aloud or in the silence of
our hearts.

Pause

We gather up these prayers in the name of the One who accepted
the cross and its shame for our sake, Jesus Christ. Amen.

TAIZÉ CHANT

Stay with me,
remain here with me,
watch and pray,
watch and pray.

MEDITATION

We watch in horror as, blow by blow, the nail is driven into his hand. Why do we recoil, in particular, at the desecration of a hand, at the sight of these hands, pierced, torn, bleeding? Perhaps it is that our hands are so primary a means of reaching out to those around us. Stretching out our hands to touch another is surely one of our earliest and most intimate gestures: we see a child reaching up, leaning toward a parent, and the lovely, arcing gesture of the parent's response, bending toward the child. And this grace of touch remains with us throughout our earthly pilgrimage: the carefree embrace of friends; the intimacy of covenanted love; the bending down over crib or bedside; the touch of reassurance when we are in pain or fear; the laying of hands on the sick and fevered and dying. All of these are expressions of our hunger for human, embodied touch.

And how great is the desert, how deep the dryness, of those who are never touched! To walk into our nursing homes, our shelters, our hospital wards is to enter into places where human touch is now almost entirely absorbed into the technical, the hygienic, the bureaucratic handling—not touching—of patients or clients. The loneliness of those whose wounds are touched only antiseptically must be very deep indeed.

Such loneliness, we might guess, drove the crowds toward Jesus. Along pathways and hillsides, in village streets, by the lakeshore, in the city of Jerusalem, the poor and lame, the blind and leprous and bleeding came to Jesus to be touched, to touch him, to touch only the fringe of his garments. They crowded in, these lost and least; they stretched out their hands to him: *Jesus of Nazareth, have pity on us.* And the gracious presence and action of Jesus during the whole of his life was to touch: to bend himself down to the wounds and the wounded of this earth and to lift them up. What intimacy this Son of Man has with his own, most especially with his wounded own.

And is there a greater instance of this intimacy than Jesus's response to Thomas, the disciple who hears the reports of resurrection but who will not believe without seeing and touching, without "casting" his hand—the word is the very same as the casting of nets overboard—into Christ's wounded side? Thomas wants to see the marks of the nails, but even more to touch them; he wants to see the wounded side, but even more to throw his hand into it. The rawness of this desire startles us, but Jesus responds: *Put your finger here and see my hands. Reach out your hand and put it in my side. Do not doubt but believe.* These last words have often been understood as a rebuke, but might we not hear in these words an invitation? Might not this Lord of compassion be offering yet one more tender, gracious sign of his loving his own to the end? Indeed, he meets Thomas's hunger for touch with a nearness that is so startling, so intimate, so new that the apostle can only break out in one of the highest confessions of the New Testament: *My Lord and my God!* (John 20:27–28).

All of this we recall as we see the nails pierce his hands and feet. For we are likewise our Lord's own. Each of us has our own wounds; and surely each of us longs for his touch, longs to cast ourselves into his wounds. As we see the wounds inflicted in Christ's body, may we remember also his transfigured wounds, his gracious invitation to us to cast ourselves, our sorrows and our brokenness, into those very wounds for healing.

STATION XII

Jesus Dies on the Cross

Jesus Dies on the Cross

READINGS FROM SCRIPTURE

Then Jesus, crying with a loud voice, said, "Father, into your hands I commend my spirit." Having said this, he breathed his last. When the centurion saw what had taken place, he praised God and said, "Certainly this man was innocent."

Luke 23:46–47

Silence is observed

Let the same mind be in you that was in Christ Jesus,
who, though he was in the form of God,
did not regard equality with God
as something to be exploited,
but emptied himself,
taking the form of a slave,
being born in human likeness.
And being found in human form,
he humbled himself
and became obedient to the point of death—
even death on a cross.

Philippians 2:5–8

PRAYER

Lord Christ, as we meditate on your passion, may we remember
also those for whom you died.
Hear our prayers this day:
for those who are crucified;
for those held in solitary confinement;
for all those tortured and slain by a perversion of justice;
for those executed;
for those who torture;
for those who kill.
We pray also for all those we name either aloud or in the silence of
our hearts.

Pause

We gather up these prayers in the name of the One who was a
prisoner and died between thieves, our Savior Jesus Christ.
Amen.

Silence is observed

MEDITATION

He hangs there, alone: beaten, exhausted, gasping for breath in the dust and heat and the lurid glare of the midday sun; exposed to the scorn of onlookers, the jeers and taunts, the cries of pain and anger and sorrow rising at his feet. In the midst of this he hangs there: suffering, still, silent. Time contracts to this solitary figure, this suspended moment.

It is the great and powerful mystery of our faith that Jesus Christ, the only begotten before all worlds, is among us, *as* one of us. Unique among all living, he yet lives and moves among us. Always alone, he is never alone. In life he is always surrounded, always with others: with his community of disciples; with followers, true and false; with crowds, desperate and hungry, pressing upon him. At the hour of his death he is flanked by others, hung with a criminal on either side. Just as he stood among followers and skeptics in the temple, and healed within its gates, and taught the crowds in Judea and Galilee, so in his death on Golgotha he is between the others, indeed in the very midst of them, and of us. So close is he to his fellows, so near the suffering and defiled, who cling to him or reject and revile him.

In life a friend of sinners and the lost, so also in death he descends in great humility to be simply one of the afflicted, one of the crucified, lost among the dead. Even as King and Lord, he is content to be like those who go down to the pit, one with those left for dead. As we gaze upon the scene of crucifixion, we see three bodies, condemned, hanging open-armed in their last agonies. Nothing picks out this one Jew or sets him apart in incarnate majesty. He is *for* us in this unique way: that he is utterly like us, indistinguishable from us, in our midst.

Only in hindsight, only from the great light cast over this one death from beyond death, can we pick out this one, rejected, from all those other criminals executed by the state that day. The soldiers who stand guard that day, so long ago, pass the time as soldiers have done throughout the world: talking and gossiping among themselves, tossing dice, exchanging old clothes for new. This day at the foot of death is like any other, this death like all the others. Even the disciples do not know the meaning of their Lord's words. And there is nothing by which we could distinguish him from others, no comeliness by which we would admire him. The One who stands for all is, in his life and death, only one among many.

But Jesus Christ, our present Lord, was content to be given over into sinners' hands, to be lost among the outcast, to be forgotten among the rejected, not *just* in that time and place, the Jerusalem of Caesar's day, but in our own day as well. Consider the lost and forsaken ones for whom our Lord is content to die: migrant workers; poor tenant farmers; the mother whose weary face tells us of despair; the victims of violence, armed conflict, oppression; those in pain or terror or sickness or desperate need.

All of this suffering, all of these crosses, but none of them is Christ's own. None of these sufferings and horrors is his own affliction. Christ bears *our* sins, bears them as the very Lamb of God, the innocent made to be sin for us. Yet he does not go to his cross without his disciples, without the soldiers, without the criminals, without the forsaken, without each of us. He is in the midst of them; he is in the midst of us. And this is great good news!

STATION XIII

Jesus Is Placed in the Arms of His Mother

Jesus Is Placed in the Arms of His Mother

READINGS FROM SCRIPTURE

And the child's father and mother were amazed at what was being said about him. Then Simeon blessed them and said to his mother Mary, "This child is destined for the falling and the rising of many in Israel, and to be a sign that will be opposed so that the inner thoughts of many will be revealed—and a sword will pierce your own soul too."

Luke 2:33–35

Silence is observed

A voice is heard in Ramah,
    lamentation and bitter weeping.
Rachel is weeping for her children;
    she refuses to be comforted for her children,
    because they are no more.

Jeremiah 31:15

PRAYER

> Lord Christ, as we meditate on your passion, may we remember
> also those for whom you died.
> Hear our prayers this day:
>> for all those who mourn the death of one they loved;
>> for those who hold in their arms the body of a loved one;
>> for those who feel their lives broken and shattered;
>> for those who cannot see their life beyond this death;
>> for those who cannot grieve or weep.
> We pray also for all those we name either aloud or in the silence of
> our hearts.

Pause

> We gather up these prayers in the name of the One born of Mary
> and borne by her at the end, Jesus Christ. Amen.

TAIZÉ CHANT

> Jesus, remember me,
> when you come into your kingdom,
> Jesus, remember me,
> when you come into your kingdom.

MEDITATION

We see her draw him against her body; she tucks his head beside her cheek, that tender gesture so characteristic of a mother with an infant. But in a terrible inversion of maternal solicitude, her son is no child but a man now, a man arrested as a criminal, shamed, tortured, and murdered. The body she cradles is torn and bloody; her own heart is wrenched apart. Mary's gestures—of body and spirit—link the cross to the cradle, reminding us of the foreordained arc of Jesus's life, from incarnation to passion. And we wonder: Does she recall Simeon's prophetic words, *And a sword will pierce your own soul too* (Luke 2:35)? And has she carried in her heart for all these years a prescient awareness of this death?

In this foreknowledge Mary is unique: unique among women, as her Son is unique, alone of all men God incarnate. And so the church has rightly shown Mary clothed in every honor, with gold, ermine, velvet. But Mary is also every woman—every mother, every wife, every daughter, every sister—who is vulnerable through the suffering of those she loves. Mary is the mother of the whole human race. She is Rachel, mourning in Ramah, the city of death. She lifts up her voice in the rubble of Dresden and Shiloh and Hiroshima, weeping for her children who are not. She wanders the waste places, the lost and forgotten lands, from Juba and Bor in South Sudan to the killing fields of Cambodia and the Ukraine, daring to look into the mass graves we ignore, refusing to be consoled, refusing to forget. At the edge of every slave market, before every faceless citadel of state terror and deportation, Mary stands at the foot of every Calvary, weeping for her son, for her children: the boy soldiers, the raped and brutalized girls, the soulless murderers, each one beloved by some mother, some Rachel, grieved and unconsoled.

Mary lives in every place. As with Rachel, Ramah is Mary's home. For Ramah is the name of death, the site of deportation, the place of exile and of slaughter. From Ramah the Israelites left for Babylon, victims of war, of greed and conquest. From Ramah, the Jews of Europe were driven from home and neighbors and familiar city streets for the killing fields of Poland, the death camps of Treblinka and Auschwitz. From Ramah, the Cherokees set out on foot and in broken-down wagons along the Trail of Tears, in exile from homeland and riverbanks and woodlands to a land that never would be home. From Ramah stream the Dinka and the Nuer, fleeing for their lives, pouring out from villages and street corners in South Sudan that now carry the great darkness of cruelty and of war. Every citizen on this earth knows Ramah, this city of our own folly and rage and deadly fear. Every citizen on earth knows this place; every one of us in the human family shares Mary's lamentation.

But Christ came to earth—to Ramah—for just this purpose, for just this work: to bring his matchless Light into our darkness and to take our exile and death for his very own. That is the cost of incarnation. And it is this cost that makes it possible in our exile, in our deportation and rebellion, even at the foot of our Lord's cross, to stand in hope. He is the Redeemer, the consolation in all our despair and loss, the life in all our death. Out of the tombs in Ramah, in South Sudan, in the slums and workhouses and battlefields of this whole sorry earth, before the tomb of every Lazarus, four days dead, we hear this commanding voice: *Come out!* (John 11:43). Come out and live! *This* is the gospel of Jesus Christ, the consolation of Israel, the hope of all the earth. Christ died that we might live, summoning us out of death into life. Thanks be to God!

| | | | | | | | | | | | | | | | | | | | | | | |

STATION XIV

Jesus Is Laid in the Tomb

| | | | | | | | | | | | | | | | | | | | | | | |

Jesus Is Laid in the Tomb

READINGS FROM SCRIPTURE

When evening had come, and since it was the day of Preparation, that is, the day before the sabbath, Joseph of Arimathea, a respected member of the council, who was also himself waiting expectantly for the kingdom of God, went boldly to Pilate and asked for the body of Jesus. Then Pilate wondered if he were already dead; and summoning the centurion, he asked him whether he had been dead for some time. When he learned from the centurion that he was dead, he granted the body to Joseph. Then Joseph bought a linen cloth, and taking down the body, wrapped it in the linen cloth, and laid it in a tomb that had been hewn out of the rock. He then rolled a stone against the door of the tomb. Mary Magdalene and Mary the mother of Joses saw where the body was laid.

Mark 15:42–47

Silence is observed

Then I saw a new heaven and a new earth; for the first heaven and the first earth had passed away, and the sea was no more. And I saw the holy city, the new Jerusalem, coming down out of heaven from God, prepared as a bride adorned for her husband. And I heard a loud voice from the throne saying,

> "See, the home of God is among mortals.
> He will dwell with them;
> they will be his peoples,

and God himself will be with them;
he will wipe every tear from their eyes.
Death will be no more;
mourning and crying and pain will be no more,
for the first things have passed away."

And the one who was seated on the throne said, "See, I am making all things new."

Revelation 21:1–5

PRAYER

Lord Christ, as we meditate on your passion, may we remember
also those for whom you died.
Hear our prayers this day:
for those with lives cut short;
for those who die unmourned, outliving everyone they knew
or loved;
for those who die in peace and hope;
for those who die in fear or pain or suffering;
for those who stand watch at the grave;
for those who fear the finality of this loss.
We pray also for all those we name either aloud or in the silence of
our hearts.

Pause

We gather up these prayers in the name of the One who went
down to the dust that we might rise, our living Lord, Jesus
Christ. Amen.

TAIZÉ CHANT

Jesus, remember me,
when you come into your kingdom,
Jesus, remember me,
when you come into your kingdom.

They bend over the body, supporting it, embracing it. Exhausted by grief, fending off despair, they cling to their beloved friend and teacher, anointing with their tears this shell from which life has departed. In just this way we grieve our own losses. In the face of the illness and sorrow that beset our lives—the death of a dear one after a long illness, the disintegration of a marriage or the failure of a career, the destruction of a childhood home—we seek comfort and consolation in the fragments that are left to us. We are like the people Israel, lamenting the ruin of the great temple in Jerusalem. The psalmist tells us that the people love Jerusalem's very rubble, her toppled stones, her empty sanctuary stripped of every bit of cloth and every vessel, every bowl and altar and holy thing. They grieve her ruin like a death visited upon an entire nation.

That temple was rebuilt, we remember, although destined for destruction yet again. And this destruction is true for every life and every building. But not so with Christ's body. The very body that his followers cradle is resurrected. For that body *is* the temple, the tabernacle, the heavenly Jerusalem. The resurrected Lord is the hope of each of us and of all peoples. Christ is the One who carries us in the heights and in the depths, in devastation and in health, in hope and in sorrow.

So in our sorrows we may look toward that new temple and new life. Out of the dark shadows we may look with longing toward that vision. St. John casts a blinding image of that new Jerusalem, a dazzling image built up of everything luminous and startling and precious: a new heaven and indeed a new earth; a city that appears like a bride on her wedding day, bejeweled and deeply beautiful; a tabernacle not made with hands but utterly divine; the almighty, utterly holy God, bending down to dwell with creatures; a Lamb slain yet gloriously alive, alive yet gloriously slain.

To perceive this vision is to discover our lives bent in the arc of heaven. But how hard it is to believe this vision is for us! How easy it is, in the midst of devastating loss or a deeply embedded sense of our own unworthiness, to be overcome by our despair and exhaustion. We recall another witness: Peter, the friend who knew the Lord yet three times denied him. How could he forgive himself, allow himself to be forgiven? And yet he is transformed, set free, set on fire by the death and resurrection of the friend he betrayed. And traveling, preaching, testifying to that forgiving death, he receives his own vision. In a dream he is shown that all animals are clean, and he understands that, over and against those ancient proscriptions that separate clean from unclean among animals, among humans, and among peoples, is set a new vision where all are clean. He declares that God has shown him that he should not call anyone profane or unclean.

How revolutionary is this command! We all have our own list of the unclean, the unacceptable. And our deeper temptation is still to put ourselves on that list. We are tempted to believe that we are the unforgivable, the unclean, the profane, who can never wholly receive the light of heaven.

But listen to that heavenly voice: Christ, the one despised, tortured, and killed through a defiling and shameful death, the one laid in haste in another's tomb, looks upon us and all earthly lepers. With wounded hands and feet and side, he tells each of us with healing in his voice, "Be made clean." Over and against that death he shows us heaven, that great city bathed in the light of grace, that comes down to us and establishes itself here with us. Listen to his voice: heaven is the city of the Lord God, and before him all are clean.

Let us pray:

O Lord God, our times are in your hands. You alone know in full the seasons of our lives, the days of joy and strength renewed, the night seasons of sorrow and aching loss, the quick exaltation of gifts given and received, the light restored after sickness or wrong. You encompass them in your greatness, O Lord; you alone make them small, at rest in the palm of your hand.

Bring us, we pray, into your presence where this pilgrimage of ours will end. Let this way of the cross rise up to your throne, and may we even now glimpse our little deaths turned over into life, even as your Son went down among the lost to bring up the prisoners and set them free. Make his way a blessing and guide for us, and grant us grace to be light along this way for those who have wandered away, and to welcome them home, as you have welcomed us.

All this we ask in the name of the One who is Lord of all seasons and days, the man of sorrows and Lord of glory, even Jesus Christ. Amen.

SECTION III

|||||||||||||||

Resources for Further Study

Artist's Afterword

Do not grieve or complain that you were born in a time when you can no longer see God in the flesh. He did not in fact take this privilege from you. As he says, "Whatever you have done to the least of my brothers and sisters, you have done to me."

AUGUSTINE OF HIPPO, SERMON 103

I did not set out to create a *Stations of the Cross*. I was forty years old when I encountered my first set of Stations, at St. Mary's Episcopal Church in northern Virginia, now my parish home for over thirty years. As is true in many parishes, St. Mary's prays the Stations only during Lent and Holy Week, hanging a set of Stations in the nave and offering a Stations service each Friday night during Lent as well as on Good Friday.

The Stations that St. Mary's used when I arrived were a set of color reproductions, roughly fourteen inches high. Participants prayed the service published in *The Book of Occasional Services*. I found the words—a combination of Scripture, response, and prayer, focused on Christ's suffering for our sake—immensely moving. But I was struck that the images seemed to serve merely as place markers. They were small, mounted on the wall of the nave at least twelve feet from the worshipers gathered in the central aisle. We glanced up from the service leaflet only long enough to ensure we were standing at the correct Station.

During those years I was moving toward new subjects in my teaching and my art. For many years I taught painting and drawing in a secular setting. My students and I discussed the "formal" aspects of an image—color, composition, line—but rarely, if ever, discussed narrative or meaning. Then I began to teach at Virginia Theological Seminary (a seminary of the Episcopal Church). Discussions with my students centered on the power of the visual arts in the life of faith. We talked about the ways in which an artist might explore scriptural and theological themes. We shared thoughts about using the visual arts in ministry. And we lingered in particular over the works of Rembrandt, one of the greatest visual interpreters of Scripture. Rembrandt interprets the biblical narrative not just through facial expression but through "gesture" (the artist's term for the way we hold our body). Significantly, we never find in his work a strict line between sacred and secular: Rembrandt peoples his depictions of Scripture with his friends and neighbors and, conversely, shows us the holy in his scenes of everyday life.

Along with this new direction in my teaching, I began working in new media and depicting new subjects. My earliest paintings and prints had expressed my fascination with the cityscape, with its random clutter of buildings, lightposts, signs, and shop windows. I rarely included a figure, concerned that a human narrative might distract the viewer from the city's spare and beautiful geometry. Now I felt moved to observe and depict the figure: I sketched on the street, from my car, and sometimes in organizations where unemployed women and men gathered to begin looking for work. I became particularly attuned to the ways in which a person's gesture helps to tell a life story, how the lift of a head or the slump of a shoulder conveys delight or despair. I also began to explore sculpture and the woodcut print as means of representing the figure more directly and powerfully. And, with Rembrandt as my mentor, I began to incorporate these observations into representations of scenes from Scripture.

While I had no plans to undertake a set of Stations, I made a large charcoal drawing of a standing Christ—*Ecce Homo*—as a study for a sculpture. It struck me, as I looked at this image, that it might serve as the first in a set of Stations. And I pondered whether it might be possible to make a set of Stations where the image itself, without accompanying words, might embody the experience of Jesus's journey to the cross: that relentless downward movement, physically and spiritually, from trial to tomb. With this in mind, I began a series of drawings, working for the most part across three Lenten seasons.

Some of these drawings came easily. With others I struggled, erasing and redrawing until the paper was in shreds and I needed to begin on a fresh sheet. The responses and suggestions of friends provided important support. In *Jesus Is Nailed to the Cross*, for instance, I had approached the scene from the back, with the thought that the viewer would look over the shoulder of the anonymous soldier and in some sense participate in the act of nailing. But as with many ideas, this worked better in concept than in execution. An elderly friend from St. Mary's suggested that I rotate the view; we now look *into* the face of the soldier, confronted with his—and our—complicity in his task.

As I drew, I wondered whether I might re-create these charcoal drawings in a fine print medium. Rendering the images either as etchings or as woodcuts would allow the creation of multiple images, each an original work rather than a reproduction. Debating between the two mediums, I concluded that woodcuts would better suit the rawness of the depictions. The woodcut print, in its simplest form, yields an image in black and white only. As the starkest and most direct of printmaking media, it seemed the most apt form for a set of Stations of the Cross.

That decision meant that I needed to transfer the final charcoal drawings to the wood blocks. The means available at that time were comparatively primitive. Today I would simply scan the drawing directly, and might even have the scans printed directly onto the wood blocks. But in 1998 I needed to shoot slides of each drawing, project the slide onto the block in a darkened room, and then trace an outline of the projected image onto the wood while trying not to block the projected image with the shadow of my arm as I drew.

With the bare outlines indicated, I could then "flesh out" the image in black and white paint before I began to cut into the wood. A woodcut is a relief print: the artist carves away all the areas that will remain blank in the final print, rolls ink across the surface of the wood, sets a sheet of paper directly on the block, and either rubs the paper with a wooden brayer or runs it through a press to transfer the ink from the block to the paper, creating a print that is the reverse of the image on the block. (Many readers will recognize the relief process from carving a linoleum block, a rubber eraser, or even a potato to create a printing block.)

I created the first woodcuts, the *Ecce Homo* and the *Pietà*, in 1998 and finished the set of fourteen prints by 2005. At that time I still considered the Stations primarily a form of Lenten devotion, and—as I had done with the preliminary drawings—I worked on the woodcuts primarily during Lent. Then, in 2017, I redrew and recut Station V, *The Cross Is Laid on Simon of Cyrene*. The impetus for this was twofold. First, during the year that I served as Artist in Residence and adjunct instructor at Wesley Seminary, African American students in my classes told me of the tradition that Simon, from Cyrene in modern-day Libya, might have been the same Simeon mentioned in Acts 13:1 as *Simeon who was called Niger* (Latin for *black*). They asked me to depict Simon as a dark-skinned African if I ever undertook another set of Stations. Second, in 2017 unresolved racial tensions in our country began to reemerge, and I decided it was time to rework Station V.

As I cut and inked and printed the new image of Simon of Cyrene, I was aware that my understanding of the Stations of the Cross had broadened since I had completed the set twelve years earlier. I could see the Stations as part of—and in a sense the stimulus for—my Laments, those prints and sculptures that depict the suffering we see around us: the desperation of refugees, prisoners, victims of torture and oppression; the confusion and despair we see in our hospitals, on our streets, in our own homes. For no one comes through this life untouched by sorrow. And I could see that all of these were taken up in the suffering that Christ bore and bears for us: *Surely he has borne our griefs and carried our sorrows* (Isaiah 53:4, RSV).

I began by saying that I did not set out to create a *Stations of the Cross*. But just as working on the first set of Stations helped to open my eyes to the suffering in our world, so my continuing work on the theme of lament has led me back to the Stations of the Cross. Last year I began work on a second set of Stations, different in almost every way from the first. These are paintings rather than prints, four feet high rather than two, on wood panels rather than paper, with contemporary rather than historical figures. With gold leaf as a background instead of stark white, these new Stations are contemporary icons of suffering and redemption. But both sets of Stations, the new ones as well as the ones in this volume, rise out of the same impulse: to honor Our Lord's Via Dolorosa and—in this way—to bear witness, across all seasons, to the suffering in the world around us and to our continued hope even in this weary land.

Readers are invited to visit margaretadamsparker.com for information about archival reproductions of the complete set of Stations of the Cross or to request permission to reproduce individual images. Images may not be reproduced without permission from the artist.

Preacher's Afterword

Any preacher will tell you that stepping into a pulpit is a humbling and moving task; it's dangerous work. Always I am honored to take up this task, and always I know, from the inside, how demanding and how transformative the act of preaching is. Like any work worth doing, there are theories about how to do it well. I have found sermon collections helpful and also intimidating; I have learned much from preachers' handbooks and memoirs and guides, and I have also learned when I must go it alone; I have tried the experiments all preachers fall prey to—reading texts, reading notes, giving up texts, giving up notes—and have been rescued from experiments I should have left behind safely on the shelf. Congregations make preachers, and I have been blessed by congregations, in parish and seminary, who have given me the matchless gift of their time, their ear, their great faithfulness. In the end, however, it must be holy Scripture itself that is the school for preachers. There is no substitute for the preacher sitting under the Word, hearing that claim afresh, looking with new eye at the truths Scripture would show us. The Bible is measureless richness—there is no end to the reality it evokes and blesses and brings near to us. It is this fathomless depth that calls forth prayer in the preacher. It is a sad sermon that has not awakened prayer in the preacher, sadder still if it cannot awaken prayer in the hearers.

I might say a word here about preparation for preaching, as this is a worry that seizes almost all preachers. How best to study the Bible? What commentaries to use? How long to take in note taking or research before finding the sermon's theme—and just what is this "theme" that preachers are supposed to set forth? How much self-examination is fitting for a preacher and her preparation? How much of my own life should be on display in a sermon: some or none at all? Preaching is a worrisome occupation. These questions show that preaching has its own "material" side, not entirely corresponding to an artist's use of canvas or wood block and burin, but similar all the same. There *is* craft in sermon writing, a tradition and a high art form, a popular voice, a learned style. Like any skill, it demands practice and serious discipline.

Some seminary students, I have learned over the years, are naturals in the pulpit. They step into it with authority and discover themselves at home. Everything they say has an ease and quiet command that call the congregation to attention, to real listening. But such natural poise is not, in truth, the preparation a sermon demands. It can be learned, if one is not born to it, and is commendable, but sermon preparation lies rather in "learning, marking, and inwardly digesting" the Holy Word, as an old collect has it. The aim of scholarly reading about holy Scripture, making use of commentaries and theological exegesis, is to make the text vivid and live to the touch, colorful and textured. Original languages—Greek and Hebrew, Latin too—are incomparable aids in uncovering the concreteness of the text, painting it in the proper colors. But there is great good in reading holy Scripture in modern tongues as well: Spanish or German or Mandarin or Swahili. These too are the original languages of the Christian church. The point, I believe, is to inhabit the house of Scripture, Bethlehem, the house of living bread. Preparation brings us into that house.

Once there, the sermon, I believe, should be about *gospel*; just this. Now, not every preacher or homiletician would agree with me here. Sermons are sometimes said to be concerned with the Bible and the world, or with the needs of a particular congregation, or with the upbuilding of the church, or with the daily tasks of the Christian life. I would not want to excise any of these aims, and I hope that some of the sermons, adapted in this volume as meditations, might show some of these traits, at least in modest scope. But I do not think that they are the proper goal or character of sermons. The preacher is to witness to the gospel: that, I believe, is the high calling of the sermon, its art form. It is the Good News that distinguishes a sermon from an edifying talk, or again from a brief lecture on the Bible, or on politics, or on care for the wounded of this earth. God has done something, the final thing, in this sorrowing world, and I believe as preacher I am to speak of it, to publicly give thanks for it, to exhibit that one death and rising until the Lord comes. That, I believe, is the sermon's matter. But there is a form, too, a form that expresses and exhibits the matter.

Preaching is not exhortation, not *paraenesis*. That view sets me at some odds, I know, with many fine preachers, early and late. And it is the prevailing style of much contemporary preaching, especially in the political realm. But I do not believe that a sermon urges an action upon the congregation, nor stirs up a resolute will to act in one way or another. It is rather the announcement of the Good News who is God; it is *proclamation, kerygma*. A style bearing this matter may be elevated or simple, somewhat scholarly or plain-spun, but it should be at heart an invitation: see the world this way; consider it in this light; welcome this word; give thanks. This is the sermon, form and matter, as gospel.

Now, that does not mean that the preacher delves only into the New Testament. Not at all. The Christian sermon has been immeasurably weakened by its narrow focus upon the New Testament, and within that, the Four Gospels, and at times within them, only golden verses, beloved of the preacher and her congregation. The lectionary—a marvelous gift to the preacher—guides her away from the text she believes she knows (she is wrong about that) and into the far richer fields of the whole canon, Old and New. One cannot preach Christ, I say, without the Law and the Prophets. Christ inhabits those texts, illumines them, and points through them to the redemption of the whole world, beginning at Jerusalem and radiating to the very edges of the earth. The preacher is witness of these things.

Readers of these sermons will recognize some theological voices at work there—the voices of sturdy Reformed masters such as John Calvin and Karl Barth, but also of favored scholastics, such as Thomas Aquinas or John Duns Scotus, and, I hope, of some of the urgent prophecy of our times in theology, in literature, and in global affairs. In my own theology I have hoped to learn from these teachers of the faith. But above all I have hoped to pattern myself, as much as is given me, on the intellectual form the medieval university gave the theologian: Doctor of the Sacred Page. Holy Scripture is strongly unique, I say, and I hope these sermons might give a glimpse of what an encounter with that book has taught me. We are to be daily converted to the sorrowful and oppressed of this earth: that is a lesson Scripture must teach me, again and again. But we are to learn, even more, that these worldly scars will not have the last word, will not be victorious, even in the haunts of jackals, but will bow in the end before the Lord of glory, the risen One who breaks every chain and rights every wrong. I pray these sermons might correspond to that great hope, conforming their small words to that mighty Word, and giving thanks. For in the end, thanksgiving is the final psalm, the final hymn of praise.

Recommendations for Further Reading:

An Annotated Bibliography

Works on Artists

Rembrandt was arguably the greatest visual interpreter of Scripture, and Käthe Kollwitz's works are a passionate cry against the suffering in our world. Other important artists are Albrecht Dürer and Allan Rohan Crite, who explored the passion narrative systematically with sets of images devoted to the passion, and Fritz Eichenberg, who fused religious sensibility with a passion for social justice.

REMBRANDT (1606–1666)

The Complete Etchings of Rembrandt, edited by Gary Schwarz. Dover Editions, 1994.
  With powerful passion images dating from 1645 to 1655.

Rembrandt and the Bible, by Hidde Hoekstra. Magna Books, 1990.
  Full-color illustrations with biblical text and commentary on the images.

Rembrandt's Drawings and Etchings for the Bible, by Hans Martin Rotermund. Pilgrim Press, 1969.
A comprehensive selection, with commentary on each image.

KÄTHE KOLLWITZ (1867–1945)

Prints and Drawings of Käthe Kollwitz, by Carl Zigrosser. Dover Fine Art Books, 1969.
A selection of Kollwitz's graphic work, including images that protest poverty, war, and political oppression.

ALBRECHT DÜRER (1471–1528)

Dürer's Passions, by Jordan Kantor. Harvard University Art Museums, 2000.
Reproductions of all five of Dürer's print series on the passion and an essay exploring Dürer's preoccupation with the subject across his lifetime.

FRITZ EICHENBERG (1901–1990)

Fritz Eichenberg: Works of Mercy, edited by Robert Ellsberg. Orbis Books, 1993.
A selection of Eichenberg's searing images, religious and political, many of them created for Dorothy Day and the Catholic Worker's Movement.

ALLAN ROHAN CRITE (1910–2007)

"Allan Rohan Crite's (Re)Visioning of the Spirituals" by Julie Levin Caro. In *Beholding Christ and Christianity in African American Art,* edited by

James Romaine and Phoebe Wolfskill. Pennsylvania State University Press, 2017.
Discussion of Crite's depictions of the spiritual "Were You There When They Crucified My Lord?," set in Crite's own Boston neighborhood, with a black Christ and Mary.

Sets of Stations with Accompanying Reflections

Stations: The Way of the Cross, by Daniel Berrigan and Margaret Parker. Harper and Row, 1989.
Berrigan's meditations on social injustice, paired with Parker's terra cotta relief sculptures of suffering on the streets of New York City. (Artist's note: Although we share a name, this Margaret Parker is not a relative.)

Walking the Way of Sorrows, Stations of the Cross, by Noyes Capehart and Katerina Katsarka Whitley. Morehouse, 2003.
Capehart's powerful woodcut images with reflections by Whitley.

A Walk in Jerusalem: Stations of the Cross, by John Peterson. Morehouse, 1998.
A contemporary Stations liturgy with photographs for each Station and a brief history of the Station, drawn from Peterson's experience as Dean of St. Georges College in Jerusalem.

Walk with Jesus: Stations of the Cross, by Henri Nouwen and Sr. Helen David. Orbis, 2015.
Nouwen's socially engaged meditations with David's spare colored-pencil drawings depicting suffering in our own time across the globe and in our own cities.

The Way of the Cross, the Path to New Life, by Joan Chittister and Janet
  McKenzie. Orbis, 2013.
  Full-color reproductions of McKenzie's contemplative images
  with meditations by Chittister.

Histories of the Stations of the Cross

"The Geography of Faith: Tracing the Via Dolorosa," by Jerome Murphy-
  O'Connor. *Bible Review* 12.6 (December 1996).
  A thorough overview of the history of the Stations.

Stations of the Cross: An Account of Their History and Devotional Purpose,
  by Herbert Thurston. Forgotten Books, reprinted on demand from
  1914 Burns & Oates edition.
  A classic account (a delightful example of late nineteenth-century
  piety) with maps and drawings.

Commentaries, Theological Works, and Sermon Collections

The Bible and the New York Times, by Fleming Rutledge. Eerdmans, 1999.
  Here is a preacher utterly unafraid of speaking the plain truth of
  the gospel to the politics of our day. She stands in a long line of
  prophetic preachers, and it is rousing and compelling to hear such
  a voice in today's fearful church. Those of us who hope to witness
  to the Bible's authority in matters of war and peace, poverty and
  class, bourgeois aims and emptiness will turn to Rutledge as un-
  rivaled counsel and guide.

Church Dogmatics IV/1, by Karl Barth. T&T Clark, 1956.
  This is the volume many prize above all others in the multivolume

Church Dogmatics, the greatest Protestant dogmatic since Friedrich Schleiermacher and John Calvin. This is Barth's doctrine of reconciliation, focused on the atonement. His treatment of the cross here is matchless in its power, scope, and systematic rigor. No one will agree with everything Barth says here, but everyone will find the gospel proclaimed with great originality and integrity.

Commentaries by John Calvin (available in many editions).
Calvin was noted in his day for his clarity and humanistic style, his firm grasp of the plain sense of Scripture, and his distaste for elaborate symbolic and typological reading, favored by many medieval preachers. Present-day preachers will learn many lessons from Calvin: brevity, forcefulness, confidence, and deep humility. Readers will come away from Calvin's commentaries instructed and edified, even, perhaps especially, when they are not convinced.

Deliverance to the Captives, by Karl Barth. HarperCollins, 1978.
Late in his career, Barth preached to prisoners in the Basel prison; this volume is a collection of those sermons. They are plainspoken and forceful, a wonderful example of a deeply learned intellect delivering the vivid and simple truth of the gospel. The concrete narrative of Scripture comes alive here. Barth was a master storyteller.

A Faith of Our Own and *The Essential Sermons*, by Austin Farrer. World, 1960, and Cowley, 1991, respectively.
Farrer was a twentieth-century Anglican divine, a philosopher, a biblical critic, a pastor and theologian, and a marvelous university preacher. Farrer understood modern worries about the Christian faith; he respected doubters, skeptics, and agnostics; he preached a high and confident Christian faith with eyes wide open.

Mysterium Paschale: The Mystery of Easter, by Hans Urs von Balthasar. Ignatius, 2000.
    Balthasar takes the Way of the Cross into Holy Saturday and de-velops an entire doctrine of the atonement, an entire Christology, out of that Sabbath when the "Eternal Word fell silent." This is a demanding work and a deeply rewarding one.

Preaching the Luminous Word, by Ellen Davis. Eerdmans, 2016.
    Throughout her many and powerful writings, Ellen Davis has shown Christians how to read, preach, and teach from the Old Testament—a vital task! Here in this sermon collection, Davis gives us examples of her rich homiletic voice, covering many doc-trines and occasions in life, and showing how the well-trained exegete might move better between Old Testament and New.

A Ray of Darkness, by Rowan Williams. Rowman and Littlefield, 1995.
    This sermon collection comes from one of the most accomplished and distinguished theologians in the contemporary world, Rowan Williams, the former Archbishop of Canterbury. Always he is startlingly honest, deeply reflective, and caught up short by the mystery of the Christian faith.

Sermons on the Parables, by Howard Thurman. Orbis Books, 2018.
    The long-time chaplain at Boston University, Thurman became one of the premier spiritual and moral teachers of the twentieth century. Thurman was one of the architects of the Civil Rights Movement, a man of unfliching honesty and profound humility.

Strength to Love, by Martin Luther King Jr. Harper & Row, 1963.
    The master.